Contents

Extending the Table

Extending the Table

A Guide for a Ministry
of Home Communion Serving

Mark W. Stamm

DISCIPLESHIP RESOURCES

P.O. BOX 340003 • NASHVILLE, TN 37203-0003
www.discipleshipresources.org

Cover design by Thelma Whitworth.
Interior design by PerfecType, Nashville, TN.

ISBN 978-0-88177-553-2

Library of Congress Control Number: 2008941605

Acknowledgements

I did not know the endpoint at the time, but this book began to take shape during Eastertide 1995, when I had meetings with a small group of parishioners at Trinity United Methodist Church in Roaring Spring, Pennsylvania. They wanted to be trained as home Communion servers, and I had ideas about what I wanted to teach them. They were also willing to share their thoughts about what they needed to learn, and those conversations shaped the course that I taught them.

My insights continued to take shape over the next decade, as I taught my course to various groups in Pennsylvania and in Texas. Conversation partners from Bloomsburg to Montoursville, from Harrisburg to Everett, Altoona, and Clearfield, from Houston to Dallas and Plano and on to Lubbock, all contributed to my understanding. Their enthusiasm for this ministry has encouraged me. Finally, my good friends at the United Methodist General Board of Discipleship convinced me to put these thoughts on paper. Thanks to all.

Introduction

When I hear the phrase "extending the table," it reminds me of preparing our dining-room table for a larger-than-usual gathering. At its normal length, our table seats four people, and usually that is sufficient. But when we are hosting a larger group, we need to make an adjustment. We pull the table from both ends, which opens a space in the center, where we add another section, called a leaf. Adjusted in that way, our table will accommodate six persons comfortably and a couple more if we all sit closely. My parents had an even bigger table to which they could add two leaves. Quite literally, it was an extended table. When I think of the Lord's Table, I think of a table of hospitality, a table of mission, a table that will extend to the walls of the church and beyond them if necessary. As we will see, extending the Lord's Table is necessary, and happily it is rooted in its very nature.

This book expands some of the key missional assertions presented in "This Holy Mystery: A United Methodist Understanding of Holy Communion," the teaching document adopted by the 2004 General Conference of the United Methodist Church. "This Holy Mystery" uses the phrase "extending the table" in two distinct yet related ways. The first use occurs in the section entitled "The Gathered Assembly" in the subsection "The Community Extends Itself." Here, the document discusses carrying Communion from the worship service to those members who are unable to attend it. Specifically, it says:

> The Communion elements are consecrated and consumed in the context of the gathered congregation. The Table may be extended, in a timely manner, to include those unable to attend because of age, illness, or similar conditions. Laypeople may distribute the consecrated elements in the congregation and

extend them to members who are unavoidably absent (*BOD*; ¶¶ 340.2.a.5 and 1117.9). An elder or deacon should offer appropriate training, preparation, and supervision for this important task (¶¶ 340.2.a.5 and 1117.9).[1]

The text reminds us that participation in the Lord's Supper is not a ritual action that we perform as isolated individuals; we do it with the whole church in mind, even those who cannot attend. My purpose in this book is to provide a resource that will facilitate the kind of training advocated within the document. The second use occurs in the final section of "This Holy Mystery" entitled "Extending the Table," and it informs us as well. That section discusses the relationship of Holy Communion to evangelism, to ethical Christian discipleship, and to the unity of the church, reminding us in the process that participation in Holy Communion is not an isolated event done solely for one's personal benefit and edification. Rather, Holy Communion relates to everything that Christians do.[2] I have discovered that the specific ministry of home Communion serving helps people live into that wider, extended vision.

Within this book I provide a clear description of what a layperson does in leading a home Communion visit (see chapter four). I also describe the steps that a local congregation should take in developing such a ministry (see chapter five). So, this book addresses the "how to" issues. As important as it is to demonstrate how to carry out the task, however, this book does more. Indeed, it does not take long to learn the mechanics of a home Communion visit, but I have found that serving Holy Communion often raises a whole complex of questions: questions about God's grace and its relation to the sacraments, questions about the nature of the church and its ministries, and other questions besides. For instance, people will ask, "Why do clergy preside at the Lord's Table, and what exactly is their role, anyway?" "Do we really need clergy?" "Do laypersons have anything to do besides receiving the bread and the cup?" I spend time discussing these significant historical, theological, and pastoral questions on the assumption that persons who know *why* they are doing this ministry do better work and find it more satisfying (see chapters one, two, and three).

The approach described here is fairly straightforward. For reasons that should become apparent, in the sixth chapter I also discuss some necessary limits on the concept of the extended table. I insist that extended table is not a good model for providing Communion to congregations that currently have no pastor. I summarize our work using some frequently asked questions that I have gathered while teaching this course in various locales (chapter seven). In an appendix, I describe several ways to make a home Communion set. Other appendices provide other materials needed for home Communion visits.

I have been training home Communion servers since Eastertide, 1995, when I gathered a small group of my parishioners at Trinity United Methodist Church in Roaring Spring, Pennsylvania, and began working with them to form a Communion visitation team. They taught me as well, with their questions shaping my understanding of what they needed to learn. During the previous summer, I had returned to parish ministry after spending four years in the Doctor of Theology program at Boston University (I defended my dissertation and graduated in 1995). Then as now, I was committed to the Eucharist and to sacramental renewal in general, and, indeed, my new congregation had asked for a pastor who would lead them in such a direction. But how? Sacramental renewal occurs in and through many decisions and teaching moments. It requires leadership and patience, both of which I exercise better at some occasions than I do at others. I received an important insight when, in the fall of 1994, my district superintendent asked me to prepare a memo for him that would explain and defend "this new practice" of laity taking Communion to shut-ins. (Well, for United Methodists it was relatively new in 1994.) Drawing on insights that I had gained from the work of Professor Laurence H. Stookey[3] and from other historical and theological materials, I prepared and submitted a memo that later became my initial presentation to my Trinity Church parishioners. It became the foundation of chapter three of this book. Indeed, many of the insights that I share in this book began to emerge within those initial conversations with parishioners, and they have continued to emerge as I have trained persons in a variety of settings.

All of the insights that I have gained about this ministry of the extended table are rooted in one of the primary assertions of the Liturgical Movement—that the Eucharist belongs to the whole assembly of faithful Christians and not simply to the clergy. The church has not always understood this fact, but if the table really does belong to the Lord, as we say it does,[4] then no class of church member—like the ordained—can claim it as its own. Granted, clergy have a particular stewardship to exercise in relation to the Eucharist. They are called to preside at the celebration; that is, they call the church to gather, and then they lead the assembly in the Great Thanksgiving. Conversely, they may not lead that prayer without a congregation.[5] To borrow the classic phrase from the Second Vatican Council of the Catholic Church, all faithful Christians, clergy and lay, are called to "full, conscious, and active participation" in the Lord's Supper.[6] Both Catholics and Protestants continue to explore the meanings of that phrase. Among other things, such participation requires a liturgy prayed in the vernacular, that is, in language that we normally use. So, Catholics translated their liturgy from Latin to modern English, and Methodists translated theirs as well, from the Elizabethan forms of the sixteenth century to a similar modern English. "Full, conscious, and active participation"[7] also implies a Communion liturgy that includes congregational singing, both within the Great Thanksgiving and while people are receiving the bread and cup. Congregational song does its deepest work when it is also expressed in the cultural heart language of the people, although we should not privilege one form of music to the exclusion of others. We should not be playing musical chairs at the Lord's Table, removing chairs so that, ultimately, only the most assertive find a place.

As "This Holy Mystery" asserts, laity may also participate in the serving of the elements, an experience that has led to a deeper sacramental engagement for many. For centuries, Catholics and many Protestants had allowed only the ordained clergy to handle the consecrated elements, to the point that the pastor served himself and rarely had the privilege of hearing someone say to him, "the body of our Lord Jesus Christ."[8] In many of our congregations, altar guilds and Communion stewards (usually women) had prepared the bread and cup(s), filling trays and sometimes arranging them on the chancel rail.[9] This ministry formed many persons in profound ways and is missed in many places where other methods of serving the elements, such as intinction, are now practiced. Nevertheless, laypersons had rarely given the consecrated bread and cup to others and had not been privileged to say the words of delivery. That practice began to change, however, when congregations moved to a common loaf and cup, often received by intinction, and when they also rediscovered the value of receiving Communion while standing.[10] Thus, I remember the reticence expressed by one young adult when, in 1983, I first asked her to administer the cup during the congregation's Communion service. "Are you sure that I can do this?" she asked. I assured her that doing so was perfectly acceptable. Later, she told me that serving her sisters and brothers had moved her deeply.

I have witnessed similar dynamics in and around home Communion serving. At first, people may not be certain that their participation in such a ministry is proper, but when they do it, many find it a grace-filled experience. I would be remiss were I to say that all resistance dissipates through practice, but the experience of a deeper Communion often sweeps most resistance away. Such experiences convince me that calling laity to serve

Communion, both within and beyond the congregation, is an important pathway toward a deeper appreciation of the sacrament. To support this assertion, in the interlude between chapters four and five, I provide testimonies from some experienced home Communion servers.

As I have said, the instruction provided here focuses on a particular task. I am teaching laity how to lead a home Communion visit while also teaching them about the foundations of the practice. To my delight, I have discovered that such a task-based focus encourages participants to better grasp the theological and historical issues. The fact that a task-based approach is an effective way for laity to learn about the sacraments should not surprise us, however, since Jesus commanded us to "do this" (1 Corinthians 11:23-26; Luke 22:19) and not merely to think about it. We might expect that our best thinking will occur in and through the doing. In order to facilitate the process of teaching and learning, I have provided discussion questions for each chapter and a short guide for persons who will lead the study of this book.

Welcome to the process of extending the table. We will begin by discussing why we need such a ministry in the first place.

Notes

1. "This Holy Mystery, A United Methodist Understanding of Holy Communion," *The Book of Resolutions of the United Methodist Church*, 2004, page 910. Copyright © 2004, The United Methodist Publishing House, used by permission. The full section covers pages 910 to 913.

BOD refers to *The Book of Discipline of the United Methodist Church*, 2004 (Nashville: The United Methodist Publishing House, 2004).

2. "This Holy Mystery," 923-930.

3. Laurence H. Stookey, *Eucharist, Christ's Feast in the Church* (Nashville: Abingdon Press, 1993), 136-143, 155-159.

4. For a discussion of this phrase and its implications, see my book *Let Every Soul Be Jesus' Guest* (Nashville: Abingdon Press, 2006), especially chapter five.

5. Mark W. Stamm, *Sacraments and Discipleship, Understanding Baptism and the Lord's Supper in a United Methodist Context* (Nashville: Discipleship Resources, 2001), 92-95.

"This Holy Mystery," 907-909.

6. *Constitution on the Sacred Liturgy*, Chapter 1, II.14 <http://www.vatican.va/archive/hist_councils/ii_vatican_council/documents/vat-ii_const_19631204_sacrosanctum-concilium_en.html>. Accessed December 28, 2007.

7. Ibid.

8. For example, see *The Book of Worship for Church and Home* (Nashville: The Methodist Publishing House, 1964), 21. The rubric reads, "*The Minister shall first receive the Holy Communion in both kinds, and then shall deliver the same to any who are assisting him.*"

9. Susan J. White, *A History of Women in Christian Worship* (Cleveland, OH: The Pilgrim Press, 2003), 179-80.

10. Receiving Communion while standing and moving in a continuous line is often presented as a time-saving method and so it is. Indeed, kneeling in groups, or "tables," and giving a separate table dismissal to each group was a common Methodist practice dating to the time of John Wesley, yet it unnecessarily lengthens Communion services. Cutting that time became a more urgent issue when larger congregations began holding Communion services more frequently than once a quarter. Nevertheless, standing for Communion is far more than a pragmatic measure. Standing is also a sign of the Resurrection, of which we are given a foretaste in the breaking of the bread (Luke 24:35).

1

Why Do We Need This Ministry?

Stories About Matters Forgotten

Those of us who teach worship courses have a cache of stories about liturgical faux pas that we enjoy sharing. It is one of the guilty pleasures of our guild. Like all good parents who truly care for their children, we exercise some discretion in telling them. Some stories we tell only late at night amidst a tight circle of confidants—after all, there are some things that we don't want the children to hear until they're older. Some we tell primarily for their entertainment value.

The best of these stories are cautionary tales with an implied moral—like the time I was helping to prepare the Perkins Chapel altar before a service for our graduating seniors and discovered that we had no bread for the Eucharist except for a few moldy and wet tortillas whose best days had been spent in the sacristy refrigerator. That's a problem when the service begins in twenty minutes. What to do? I sent one person out to buy bread, while another took it upon herself to run a similar errand; finally, the person who was supposed to bring the bread showed up late, but with loaf in hand. By the time the sermon began, I was sitting on the back row of Perkins Chapel holding three rather large loaves of bread and trying to suppress my giggles. It was a multiplication of bread in our little wilderness, and I hadn't even spoken a blessing, at least not one that I could repeat in public. During the passing of the peace, I deftly moved one large loaf to the altar, left another on the credence table just in case, and made plans to eat the third loaf at home. Thus, when the presider removed the altar veil, the paten was not bare. We liturgists know how to figure out these situations, and that's why we make the big bucks.

Sometimes we tell real horror stories. A colleague of mine served as the interim pastor of a large urban congregation, a place where preaching was the primary focus and efficiency was highly valued. To his dismay, he discovered that the service of Holy Communion had not been offered in their principal service for several years. Why? They said it took too much time. It produced too much dead air for the weekly television broadcast, and the logistics were too complicated. My colleague assured them that they could work through those challenges, and moreover that they needed to do so. Thus regular offerings of the Lord's Supper resumed. I have often wondered what I would have done had I been a member of that congregation. Perhaps some people did complain about the former pastor's dereliction of duty but were unable to overcome the power distance between the pastor and themselves. Perhaps some left there and went to other congregations. In all likelihood, most members simply adjusted to an unbalanced spiritual diet and tried to make the best of a bad situation. We can assume that God continued to work in that place, ministering through the means of grace that were available.[1] Nevertheless, it was not an ideal situation. Jesus told his disciples to feed the crowd, saying, "You give them something to eat" (Luke 9:13). In this case, the disciples refused.

Like the members of that congregation, many Christians find themselves without Holy Communion for varied periods of time, yet their problem is not as noticeable. Some live in nursing homes, and others are hospitalized temporarily. Others are not able to leave their homes due to illness or disability, and others can no longer abide crowds. Some work in those hospitals and nursing homes, and others care for people who cannot leave home. Others— various types of service workers, police officers, fire-fighters, military personnel, and truck drivers—must work on Sundays, sometimes far from home. Some church members are incarcerated. The church takes Communion to some of these on a regular basis; it forgets others.

Does it really matter? Why was it a serious problem when that pastor stopped offering the Lord's Supper at the principal service in that congregation? Why do our unwillingly absent members need Communion? For that matter, why does anyone need it?

Holy Communion as a Formative Encounter with the Living Christ

The church has always believed that its members need Holy Communion, and thus it has always celebrated it. This sacrament remains at the heart of what we do. We gather for the Eucharist believing that we encounter the living Christ in the midst of it. "The bread that we break," the Apostle Paul asked the Corinthian church, "is it not a sharing in the body of Christ?" (1 Corinthians 10:16). Granted, he said that while he was rebuking that congregation for their misshapen practice of the holy meal, but they needed to get it right because it was vital to their live in Christ. Misuse would lead to malformation. Their transgressions were particularly serious because they were doing them in the Lord's presence, to the Lord's people, his body (see especially 1 Corinthians, chapters 11 and 12).

The earliest Christians normally gathered for the Lord's Supper on the Lord's Day, that is, on Sunday or "the first day of the week" (Luke 24:1).[2] It was the weekly commemoration of the Lord's Resurrection where they encountered Christ's presence "in the breaking of the bread" (Luke 24:35).[3] The Emmaus Road narrative (Luke 24:13-35) functions as an icon of the church's experience. To speak of its iconic value is not to question the historical foundations of that narrative;[4] nevertheless, one may hear it as a reflection of the church's experience at the time that the third Gospel was written, approximately fifty years after that first Easter. On Sundays, the "same day" that Christ had risen (Luke 24:1, 13), he met the gathered disciples on the road, in the midst of their life's journey. As always, their lives were full of challenges and disillusioning events (Luke 24: 13-14). Within the assembly, the scriptures were read and interpreted in the light of Christ, and this Word moved their hearts, as if Christ were speaking with them directly (Luke 24:32). As Jesus had done, they "took bread, blessed and broke it, and gave it to" one another (Luke 24: 30). As they shared that meal, "their eyes were opened" (Luke 24:31), and they were able to see the world in a renewed way. Jesus was redeeming it, and they were part of what he was doing. Indeed, the Risen Christ was "made known to them in the breaking of the bread" (Luke 24:35).

The continuing encounter at the Eucharist shaped the Body of Christ. Ignatius of Antioch, a church leader from early in the second century, believed that participation in it was essential. He complained about a faction that had developed "strange doctrine touching the grace of Jesus Christ."[5] They stopped caring about those who were suffering. He wrote, "They have no care for love, none for the widow, none for the orphan, none for the afflicted, none for the prisoner, none for the hungry or thirsty."[6] How had this happened?

> They abstain from eucharist (thanksgiving) and prayer, because they allow not that the eucharist is the flesh of our Saviour Jesus Christ, which suffered for our sins, and which the Father of His goodness raised up.[7]

For Ignatius, the encounter with Christ in the Eucharist was the source of compassion.

This connection is witnessed in other places as well. Justin Martyr, a mid-second-century interpreter of church life at Rome, reported that Christians offered bread and wine for the celebration of the Eucharist, but that they also offered other gifts for distribution to the poor.[8] Eucharist and mission were linked. The fifth-century saint, Augustine of Hippo, insisted that when the church offered the bread and cup on the altar, they were indeed offering themselves. They saw there the sign of what they were becoming by grace, the Body of Christ,[9] and they became part of his ongoing mission to the world. These and other witnesses reflect the church's conviction that participation in the Eucharist was a saving and life-giving reality both for participants and for others. John Wesley stood within this stream of teaching.

John Wesley and the Lord's Supper as a Means of Grace

John Wesley believed that Christian conversion was an ongoing process. The Holy Spirit worked in people well before they were aware of it, drawing them toward active faith in Christ. He called this dynamic prevenient grace, that is, "the grace that goes before." Such grace is:

> . . . all the 'drawings' of 'the Father'; the desires after God, which, if we yield to them, increase more and more;—all that light wherewith the Son of God "enlighteneth every one that cometh into the world": showing every man "to do justly, to love mercy, and to walk humbly with his God."[10]

As one continued seeking, eventually one came to a living faith in Christ. Sometimes that faith was realized in an instant, at which time a person knew that he or she had been forgiven. Wesley testified to such an event in his famous account of the May 24, 1738, meeting on Aldersgate Street, London:

> In the evening I went very unwillingly to a society in Aldersgate Street, where one was reading Luther's Preface to the Epistle to the Romans.

About a quarter before nine, while he was describing the change which God works in the heart through faith in Christ, I felt my heart strangely warmed. I felt I did trust in Christ, Christ alone for my salvation: And an assurance was given me, that he had taken away my sins, even mine, and saved me from the law of sin and death.[11]

He called this grace of the awakened heart "justifying grace," that work of God that brings one pardon for sin. He insisted, however, that God wants to do considerably more, to bring persons to a holiness of heart and life that reflects God's nature. He called this movement of the Spirit "sanctifying grace." He wrote:

There is a *real* as well as *relative* change. We are inwardly renewed by the power of God. We feel the "love of God shed abroad in our heart by the Holy Ghost which is given unto us"; producing love to all mankind, and more especially to the children of God; expelling the love of the world.[12]

Wesley did not leave this discussion of grace in the abstract; rather he developed a structure of classes and a set of guidelines to help Methodists receive it. Receiving the Lord's Supper stood at the heart of this system.

These guidelines, published in 1743, were called "The General Rules for the United Societies."[13] One was expected to demonstrate one's desire for spiritual progress—or, in Wesley's words, "a desire to flee from the wrath to come, to be saved from their sins"[14] by observing the following three rules: (1) Doing no harm, (2) Doing good, and (3) Attending upon the ordinances of God.[15] He offered a specific list of practices under each of the rules. Under the third rule, he listed the following practices:

The public worship of God; the ministry of the Word either read or expounded; the supper of the Lord; family and private prayer; searching the Scriptures; and fasting or abstinence.[16]

In other writings, he joined his Anglican tradition in referring to these practices as "the means of grace." He insisted that Christians were duty bound to observe these practices—the Lord's Supper among them—and to promote their use. Without them, one could expect little spiritual progress.[17]

His most forceful arguments in support of the Lord's Supper were expressed in his 1732 sermon "The Duty of Constant Communion," a text included in the study edition of "This Holy Mystery."[18] According to the rubrics in force during Wesley's lifetime, members of the Church of England were expected to receive Communion three times a year, "of which Easter [was] to be one."[19] As often happens when minimum requirements are expressed, they can become the *de facto* rule, so some parishes offered Communion but three times a year. In other places where the sacrament was available on a weekly basis, attendance was often poor and eucharistic discipline lax. A variety of factors contributed to this pattern, but we should consider one in particular because echoes of it remain with us. In the piety of the late medieval period, most Catholic laypeople had received Communion but once a year, on Easter;[20] and, Wesley wrote this sermon less than two hundred years after the emergence of the English Reformation. Practice changes slowly, because the piety that supports practice is deeply rooted. Indeed, when one views thrice-annual Communion over against the old practice of annual reception, receiving three times a year may have seemed quite frequent, even excessive. Continuing concerns about one's worthiness to receive the sacrament discouraged others from participating, and still others simply did not value Communion all that much. Some were not very religious, and others had found more satisfying devotional practices.

Such was the situation addressed by John Wesley, yet he insisted that one fact overshadowed all others and overruled all of the objections: Jesus had commanded "Do this in remembrance of me."[21] He argued that "frequent" was not an adequate word; as we have seen, for some, receiving three or four times a year seemed quite frequent. He said that we should seek "constant" Communion instead. Christians should obey Christ's command as often as they could, which, he insisted, meant weekly reception, at least.[22] Indeed, Wesley himself received Communion as often as every four or five days, and we also know that, at the founding of the American church, he urged the elders to observe the Lord's Supper each Lord's Day.[23] Hence, Wesley held the ideal of a weekly Eucharist on the Lord's Day, even though practicing it was not possible in the early days of the Methodist Episcopal Church and significant doubts have been raised as to whether English Methodists other than Wesley practiced it on a widespread basis.[24]

In all likelihood, the appeal to frequency for duty's sake would move only the most loyal church members, so Wesley offered a more persuasive argument—Communion is good for us. Christians should commune as often as possible "because the benefits . . . are so great . . . namely the forgiveness of our sins and the present strengthening of our souls."[25] He insisted that preparation for Communion is important and valuable, but that lack of preparation should not keep one from Communion. After all, Jesus had said, "Do this," so refusing his commandment for lack of preparation or for any other reason would only add to one's sin. "Do this" was the decisive word, and it meant constant Communion. While most Methodists did not receive

Communion as often as Wesley had hoped, many continued to value it highly and believed that it was an effective means of grace, even a foretaste of the heavenly banquet.[26]

If, with Wesley, we believe that receiving Holy Communion is vital to our spiritual lives, then the church is duty bound to find ways to include its unwillingly absent members in its celebrations. In continuity with John Wesley, "This Holy Mystery" reaffirms the centrality of the Eucharist for contemporary United Methodists.

"This Holy Mystery": A Call to "Something More"

"This Holy Mystery" begins with the following vignette:

> The story is told of a little girl whose parents had taken her forward to receive Holy Communion. Disappointed with the small piece of bread she was given to dip in the cup, the child cried loudly, "I want more! I want more!" While embarrassing to her parents and amusing to the pastor and congregation, this little girl's cry accurately expresses the feelings of many contemporary United Methodist people. We want more! We want more than we are receiving from the sacrament of Holy Communion as it is practiced in our churches.[27]

This story expresses a variety of important themes. (1) The fact that its subject is a child receiving Communion witnesses to a relatively new, yet widespread, consensus—that young children belong at the Lord's Table. That consensus did not exist forty years ago. (2) In the disappointment over the small piece of bread, we find a call to better ritual practice with a fuller use of sacramental signs—in this case, bigger pieces of bread. (3) The call for something more speaks to the desire for deeper theological reflection on the Eucharist. Some will also hear in this phrase a call to more frequent Communion, perhaps even the "constant Communion" envisioned by John Wesley.

The document addresses all of these issues. In characteristic Methodist style, "This Holy Mystery" presses the boundaries of inclusion ever wider, especially in the assertion that "all who respond in faith are to be welcomed." Although it affirms the historic norm of baptism as the standard for admission to the table, it makes an exception for non-baptized seekers.[28] The document affirms the emerging consensus, noted above, that baptized children should receive Communion: "The theological basis for baptism of infants and people of varying abilities applies as well to their participation in Holy Communion."[29] It also affirms Wesley's teaching on Communion as a necessary means of grace[30] and, once again, calls Methodists to practice the ancient standard of weekly Eucharist on the Lord's Day:

> The complete pattern of Christian worship for the Lord's Day is Word and Table—the gospel is proclaimed in both Word and sacrament. Word and Table are not in competition; rather they complement each other so as to constitute a whole service of worship. Their separation diminishes the fullness of life in the Spirit offered to us through faith in Jesus Christ.[31]

In making that assertion, the document cites early church practice— "The practice of the Christian church from its earliest years was weekly celebration of the Lord's Supper on the Lord's Day"[32]—as well as John Wesley's clear commitment to this ideal.[33] Anecdotal evidence shows that increasing numbers of congregations have attained that goal while many more are considering it. Although there remains much work to be done regarding Methodist practices of the Lord's Supper, the United Methodist Church stands closer to Wesley's goal of constant Communion than it has at any point since the Methodist Episcopal Church began in 1784.

The call to extend the table stands on the theological foundations noted above. In her commentary on the text, Gayle Felton quotes from an article that I wrote, saying, "Such extension might be thought of as 'the open table turned outward in pastoral care and mission.'"[34] The logic is clear. If participating in Holy Communion is essential to our spiritual growth and well-being, then the church must provide regular (if not constant!) Communion to its members who cannot attend its public services. Upon further reflection on the nature of the Christian church, the need presents itself even more clearly.

"Remember Me": Extension of the Table as Discipline Against Forgetting

When we celebrate the Lord's Supper, we follow the commandment of Jesus, who said, "Do this in remembrance of me" (Luke 22:19). What do we mean by "remembrance"? The English word is translated from the Greek *anamnesis*, a word that speaks to a reality deeper than mere reminiscence. *Anamnesis* is deeply biblical, rooted in the church's reading and proclamation of the Word. We recall and proclaim the saving acts of God and especially the life, death, and resurrection of Jesus. Prayers in the Hebraic tradition, like the Great Thanksgiving, begin by proclaiming what

God has done. Petition emerges from *anamnesis* (for biblical examples of such prayers, known as *berakah*, or "blessings," see Genesis 24:27; Exodus 18: 10-11; 1 Kings 8: 56-61). When New Testament texts speak of Jesus taking bread and blessing it (e.g., Mark 6:41; 14:22), they refer to this type of prayer. For example, in such prayers, the faithful would remember God's deliverance of Israel from bondage not merely as a wistful memory, but rather as a bold prayer that God would do such a thing again. In like manner, when we gather at the Lord's Table in remembrance of Christ, we do so praying that the one who "healed the sick, fed the hungry, and ate with sinners"[35] will join us sinners yet again, bring healing grace to us, and use us to feed others. *Anamnesis* is strong, bold prayer rooted in God's covenant promises.

Our relationships within the covenant move us to a slightly different, yet related kind of remembering. In the spirit of the petition made by the thief on the cross, we ask Jesus, "Remember me when you come into your kingdom" (Luke 23:42), that is, "save us and work in our lives." As members of the Body of Christ, we are called to participate in both kinds of remembering. We remember the mighty acts of God, and thereby we pray more boldly. We also join Christ in remembering our sisters and brothers in the church. If we lose even one of them, then we lose a part of ourselves, diminishing the Body. Their pain is ours also, for we are one; so we reach out to them in compassion, becoming an answer to their prayers. Such remembering is the kind of work St. Paul was urging the Corinthian church to do when he said, "So then, my sisters and brothers, when you come together to eat, wait for one another" (1 Corinthians 11:33). Thus, when we gather together, we should ask ourselves, "Who is missing?" The question has both missional and pastoral implications, and it demands specific responses. Are the young adults missing? Why? What about the Latino/a families that recently moved into the neighborhood? Are they missing? What about Rebecca, who is at home caring for her mother with Alzheimer's disease? Is she missing? What should we do about it? What about Mr. Smith, who used to come to church every week but now resides in a nursing home? And so on. The church will never be fully gathered, but we should continue to ask the question, "Who is missing?" Asking this question on a regular basis is an important spiritual discipline for the whole church.

Forgetting is all too easy, even when we have the best of intentions. Today, I live in a rapidly growing suburb north of Dallas, Texas, in a county whose population has more than doubled in the last fifteen years. People and businesses come and go; subdivisions spring up seemingly overnight, and the highway department is constantly building and repairing roads. Church membership rolls seem to change just as quickly. In contrast, I served my last parish appointment before I moved to Perkins School of Theology in a relatively small mill town in rural central Pennsylvania. In this stable community, change seemed to occur slowly, and the church reflected the community. I served a congregation of approximately four hundred members. On average, we gained about ten members a year, through transfers and professions of faith, and lost about the same number, through death, transfer, and withdrawal. In an average year, our membership changed by about twenty persons, or about five percent. Many of our congregations are like that, seemingly stable with minimal change year to year. But if one projects a similar rate of change over a longer term, a different picture emerges. Over five years such a congregation would change by about twenty-five percent, and in a decade its membership would change by as much as half. Test this dynamic in your congregation, and see what you discover. Change is inevitable, and it occurs more rapidly than we may realize.

Imagine what that dynamic means for an elderly person, perhaps once an active and vital member of the church, who arrives at the point where she can no longer attend public services. If the church is not diligent, it can easily forget her, especially if some of her significant peers have died and her children have moved away. In all likelihood, her pastor will place her name on the church shut-in list and will visit her on a regular basis; yet visits by the pastor are not enough, for the pastor is not the whole church. While the pastor's visits are important, our shut-in matron needs fellowship with others in the church, and they need to make a connection with her as well, for together they are the Body of Christ. Together, God calls them to remember what Christ has done, to remember one another, and to share their wisdom. Extended table is a discipline that keeps congregations from forgetting their members, and that is why laypersons in congregations of all sizes need to participate in it.

There is blessing in the remembering. When I was about five years old and living in another small Pennsylvania town, my father, who was a pastor, took me along on a home visit. We went to see Ms. Cynthia Andrews. Ms. Cynthia was not able to leave home and was quite hard of hearing. I wondered, had she always been sitting in her little house hardly able to move or hear? I soon learned otherwise. She couldn't hear much, but she told great stories. She took out an old album and showed me photographs of another little house, a log house that once had been her home. It was located in rural Wyoming, where she had taught school as a much younger woman. In those days, she rode her horse to school. She showed me another photograph, and there she was—Ms. Cynthia seated on a horse, upright in the saddle with a satchel filled with books, a one-woman cavalry against ignorance. When I met her, she couldn't move much anymore, but the adventure of those earlier days was alive in her heart. She still loved to teach, and I was her newest student. She moved into a nursing home not long after I met her, and I visited her there several more times before she died.

We lose stories like this one when we no longer visit one another, and we miss opportunities to learn the deep history of our congregations. There is a blessing in remembering one another; but, blessing or not, we are the Body of Christ, members of one another. We have an obligation to visit one other.

Questions for Discussion

Take note of the questions that Gayle Felton presents in the Discipleship Resources study edition for "This Holy Mystery," pages 26-28.

Share your most memorable experience of Holy Communion. In what ways has the Lord's Supper been a means of grace to you and your congregation? In what ways are you looking for "something more"?

How often does your congregation celebrate the Lord's Supper? How is the schedule devised? What would it be like to practice the "constant Communion" that Wesley advocated?

Look around your congregation and community. How do you respond to the question, "Who's missing"?

Does your church have a home Communion list? What is the procedure for placing a person on it, and who is responsible for administering it? Who visits those on the list, and how often is that done? When was it last reviewed and updated? How could the church improve this process?

Notes

1. For a discussion of the concept of "power distance," see the book by Eric H.F. Law, *The Wolf Shall Dwell with the Lamb: A Spirituality for Leadership in Multicultural Communities* (St. Louis: Chalice Press, 1993), 22, 25.

2. *Didache*, chapter 14, in *Early Christian Fathers*, Cyril C. Richardson, editor,

in collaboration with Eugene R. Fairweather, Edward Rochie Hardy, and Massey Hamilton Shepherd (New York: Collier Books, 1970), 178.

Justin Martyr, *First Apology*, chapter 67 in *Liturgies of the Western Church*, selected and introduced by Bard Thompson (Philadelphia: Fortress Press, 1961), 9.

3. Eventually, the calendar expanded to include celebrations of the Eucharist on other days of the week. Anniversaries of the deaths of saints and martyrs became occasions for the holy meal because they, also, shared in the Paschal Mystery of Christ's dying and rising; but Sunday remained the principal day.

4. Eugene LaVerdiere, *Dining in the Kingdom of God, The Origins of the Eucharist in the Gospel of Luke* (Archdiocese of Chicago: Liturgy Training Publications, 1994), 155.

5. Ignatius of Antioch, "To the Smyrnaeans," 6, in *The Apostolic Fathers, Comprising The Epistles (genuine and spurious) of Clement of Rome, The Epistles of S. Ignatius, The Epistle of S. Polycarp, The Martyrdom of S. Polycarp, The Teaching of the Apostles, The Epistle of Barnabas, The Shepherd of Hermas, The Epistle to Diognetus, The Fragments of Papias, The Reliques of The Elders Preserved in Irenaeus*, revised texts with short introductions and English translations, by the late J. B. Lightfoot, D.D., D.C.L., LL.D., Lord Bishop of Durham, Edited and Completed by J. R. Harmer, M.A., Fellow of Corpus Christi College, Cambridge, Sometime Chaplain to the Bishop. Published by the Trustees of the Lightfoot Fund (London and New York: Macmillan and Co., 1891), 158.

6. Ibid.

7. Ibid.

8. *Liturgies of the Western Church*, selected and introduced by Bard Thompson (Philadelphia: Fortress Press, 1961), 9.

9. Augustine of Hippo, Sermon 272, quoted in *Documents of Christian Worship, Descriptive and Interpretive Sources*, James F. White, editor (Louisville, Kentucky: Westminster/John Knox Press, 1992), 192.

10. John Wesley, "The Scripture Way of Salvation," *The Works of John Wesley*, Volume 6 (Grand Rapids, Michigan: Zondervan Publishing House, produced from an 1872 edition), 44.

11. Journal, May 24, 1738, *The Works of John Wesley*, Volume 1 (Grand Rapids, Michigan: Zondervan Publishing House, produced from an 1872 edition), 103.

12. John Wesley, "The Scripture Way of Salvation," 45.

13. See discussion of the General Rules in my earlier books, *Sacraments and Discipleship, Understanding Baptism and the Lord's Supper in a United Methodist Context* (Nashville: Discipleship Resources, 2001), 19-21 and *Let Every Soul Be Jesus' Guest, A Theology of the Open Table* (Nashville: Abingdon Press, 2006), 140-42.

14. John Wesley, "The Nature, Design, and General Rules of the United Societies in London, Bristol, Kingswood, and Newcastle upon Tyne (1743)," in *The Works of John Wesley*, Volume 9, *The Methodist Societies: History, Nature, and Design*, edited by Rupert E. Davies (Nashville: Abingdon Press, 1989), 69.

15. John Wesley, "The Nature, Design, and General Rules," 71-73.

16. Ibid., 73.

17. John Wesley, "The Means of Grace," *The Works of John Wesley, Volume I, Sermons I, 1-33,* edited by Albert C. Outler (Nashville: Abingdon Press, 1984), 376-97.

18. See appendix in Gayle Carlton Felton, *This Holy Mystery, A United Methodist Understanding of Holy Communion* (Nashville: Discipleship Resources, 2005), 65-70.

19. *The Book of Common Prayer* website, <http://justus.anglican.org/resources/bcp/>. 1662 *The Book of Common Prayer*, "The Order for the Administration of the Lord's Supper, Holy Communion." <http://www.eskimo.com/~lhowell/bcp1662/communion/index.html>. Accessed October 2, 2006.

20. Eamon Duffy, *The Stripping of the Altars, Traditional Religion in England 1400-1580* (New Haven: Yale University Press, 1992), 60.

21. John Wesley, "The Duty of Constant Communion," *The Works of John Wesley,* Volume 7 (Grand Rapids, Michigan: Zondervan Publishing House, produced from an 1872 edition), 147, 150 (¶ I.1-2, etc.; ¶ II.3, 5-6).

Throughout the sermon, Wesley continues to remind the readers that "do this" is a commandment that Christians are duty bound to obey.

22. Ibid., 149-50, 156 in *Works,* Volume 7.

23. *John Wesley's Prayer Book: The Sunday Service of the Methodists in North America,* with introduction, notes, and commentary by James F. White (Cleveland, OH: OSL Publications, 1991). September 9, 1784, letter, non-numbered page opposite page A-2.

24. Henry D. Rack, *Reasonable Enthusiast, John Wesley and the Rise of Methodism* (Nashville: Abingdon Press, 1989, 1992), 418-19.

25. John Wesley, "The Duty of Constant Communion," 148 (¶ I.2).

26. Lester Ruth, *A Little Heaven Below, Worship at Early Methodist Quarterly Meetings* (Nashville: Kingswood Books, 2000), 145-54, 214-15.

The Wesley brothers taught that the Lord's Supper was, among other things, a foretaste of the heavenly banquet. See J. Ernest Rattenbury, *The Eucharistic Hymns of John and Charles Wesley,* American edition, Timothy J. Crouch, O.S.L., editor (Akron, Ohio: OSL Publications, 1990, 1996), 183-89.

27. "This Holy Mystery, A United Methodist Understanding of Holy Communion," *The Book of Resolutions of the United Methodist Church,* 2004, page 884. Copyright © 2004, The United Methodist Publishing House, used by permission.

28. Ibid., 900.

29. Ibid., 902.

30. Ibid., 890-891.

31. Ibid., 905.

32. Ibid.

33. Ibid.

34. Gayle Carlton Felton, *This Holy Mystery, A United Methodist Understanding*

of Holy Communion (Nashville: Discipleship Resources, 2005), 38. Used by permission.

The Stamm quotation comes from "'Do This.' Thoughts on the Reception and Implementation of 'This Holy Mystery'" in *Sacramental Life* 16:4 (Fall 2004), 818-819.

35. *The United Methodist Hymnal* (Nashville: The United Methodist Publishing House, 1989), 9.

From "A Service of Word and Table I" © 1972, 1980, 1985, 1989, The United Methodist Publishing House. Used by permission.

2

How Have We Practiced This Ministry in the Past?

Home Communion serving by United Methodist lay members began officially with the approval of *The United Methodist Book of Worship* by the 1992 General Conference. With that action, "A Service of Word and Table V with Persons Who Are Sick or Homebound" became part of the official ritual of the church.[1] Actually, *The Book of Discipline* itself made no specific reference to lay administration of home Communion until the following provision was included in the 1996 book:

> Ordained elders may select and train lay members with appropriate words and actions to immediately deliver the consecrated communion elements to members confined at home, in a nursing home, or in a hospital.[2]

In the current version of the 2004 *Discipline*, the provision is more open-ended. As part of her/his ministry of administering the sacraments, the pastor is expected "to select and train deacons and lay members to serve the consecrated Communion elements,"[3] although the *Discipline* does not say exactly where they should serve them, or when.

Home Communion serving by laypersons is a new practice for United Methodists. When we take an historical and ecumenical perspective, however, we see that extended table represents a restoration of an ancient

Christian practice, a restoration that is occurring within the United Methodist Church and in other denominations, including the Roman Catholic Church.

How have Christians practiced this ministry of home Communion serving in the past? I will begin to address this question by surveying some key witnesses from the first several centuries of the church. Then in the second section I will review some key developments from late medieval Catholicism along with some corrections made by Protestant reformers. As we shall see, those corrections shaped home Communion practices until the developments represented by the recent changes in the United Methodist rubrics. In the final section of the chapter, I will offer a cautionary word about those recent changes.

Witnesses From the Early Centuries

The First Apology of Justin Martyr, written around 150 CE, contains the earliest known reference to Communion offered beyond the congregational service. Justin described the pattern of Sunday worship followed by his congregation in Rome. The service proceeded from the gathering to the reading of scripture followed by a sermon in which "the president verbally instructs and exhorts to the imitation of these good things."[4] After the sermon, the congregation would rise and offer its prayers. The author then provided the following description of the Eucharist:

> . . . bread and wine and water are brought, and the president in like manner offers prayers and thanksgivings, according to his ability, and the people assent, saying Amen; and there is a distribution to each, and a participation of that over which thanks have been given, and to those who are absent a portion is sent by the deacons. And they who are well to do, and willing, give what each thinks fit; and what is collected is deposited with the president, who succours the orphans and widows, and those who, through sickness or any other cause, are in want, and those who are in bonds, and the strangers sojourning among us, and in a word takes care of all who are in need.[5]

Within this description one finds witness to an offering of gifts, to a free-form eucharistic prayer with the "amen" of the congregation, and to Communion of the gathered congregation. Then we hear about several important extensions of that gathering. First, Communion was sent to "those who are absent," a category that could include the infirm, those in prison, those who were working, as well as others. We also hear about their support for persons in need and sojourners. Indeed, "This Holy Mystery" uses the phrase "extending the table" to refer to both types of outreach: the extension of Holy Communion to the homebound[6] as well as the broad missional impulse rooted in the Eucharist.[7] In this chapter, I will limit myself to a discussion of extended *Communion*, although it is always good for us (and our congregations) to remember and practice both types of extension.

We cannot determine whether the practice of extension described in *First Apology* occurred in most congregations. Because sources describing worship during the first three centuries of the church are rare, contemporary liturgical scholars have been increasingly reluctant to generalize them.[8] We can claim, however, that Justin's congregation in Rome practiced a ministry of extended Communion and that his description of worship has had a major influence on contemporary practices.

We admire the pastoral practice described in *First Apology*, and thus we imitate it. Nevertheless, the sending of previously consecrated elements to absent members did open a slight gap between the prayer of thanksgiving and the receiving of Communion, and that gap would develop along some unfortunate trajectories in later centuries. The text known as *The Apostolic Tradition of Hippolytus* presents evidence of a widening in that gap. It called believers to receive the Eucharist early in the morning before eating anything else[9,] and it also called the faithful to protect the Eucharist against being consumed by mice or by unbelievers.[10] Why include these rubrics? We should not imagine vermin-infested altar-tables, nor must we necessarily assume that the entire assembly fasted before the Lord's Day Eucharist. Rather, it appears that individual Christians were given some of the consecrated bread to take home following the Lord's Day celebration, portions of which they received when they offered their prayers at the beginning of each day. Since they were keeping the sacrament at home, they needed rubrics to protect it against misuse by unbelievers, not to mention vermin.[11]

While scholars once believed that *The Apostolic Tradition* was a third-century Roman document, many scholars now believe that the document developed over several centuries and in several locales. It is living literature, reflecting developing traditions.[12] Other witnesses, however, suggest that some third-century Christians in North Africa were allowed to take consecrated bread home and receive it during the week.[13] While that practice of self-administered home Communion did not long survive, especially as lay

Communion became less frequent during the centuries following the legalization of Christianity, the practice of reserving Communion for the sick continued. Why did the practice of reservation develop? According to W.H. Freestone, persecution made reservation necessary:

> The method of distribution during or immediately after the public service would lead on almost insensibly to the habit of reservation; since in cases where it was impossible or inconvenient to carry forth the sacrament at once (as might often happen during the persecutions) some temporary mode of reserving would be inevitable.[14]

When I speak of "reservation," I am referring to the practice of retaining some of the consecrated elements (usually the bread) at the conclusion of the Eucharist and storing it in a dignified and protected place within the church building until it was needed. A small box or container called a *pyx* would be used for storage and transport, and it would be removed when *viaticum*, literally "food for the journey," was needed. *Viaticum* was Communion provided to persons who were dying.

Reservation and administration took various forms. Some monks carried the sacrament with them at all times, perhaps in a small container called a *capsa* worn around the neck so that they could offer *viaticum* whenever the need arose. In this manner, they also provided it for themselves.[15] In some churches, the *pyx* might be hung in a *columba(e)*, a dove-shaped vessel that would be suspended over the altar.[16] As the practice and theology of reservation developed, more elaborate structures were built, called tabernacles, in which the consecrated elements were kept under lock and key. These practices were well established by the end of the first millennium.

Somewhat ironically, decline in regular lay Communion contributed to an increased need for *viaticum*, as people did not want to face death without benefit of a recent Communion. Thus, Communion was reserved in the churches for pastoral reasons so that it could be offered to people on relatively short notice. The church always treated these consecrated elements with special reverence; it was, after all, the Body of Christ. Nevertheless, theological controversies that emerged toward the end of the first millennium heightened the church's sense of obligation to the reserved sacrament and led to the development of new devotional practices. As we will see in the next section, Protestant reformers opposed these practices, and their arguments shaped Methodist developments.

Developments and Corrections

Theological and Devotional Developments

The conviction that one receives the body and blood of Christ in the Eucharist is as old as the Gospel accounts themselves. Indeed, Jesus broke the bread, gave it to the disciples, and said, "This is my body" (Mark 14:22). In the fourth Gospel, we hear Jesus say, "Those who eat my flesh and drink my blood abide in me, and I in them" (John 6: 56). As noted earlier, Ignatius of Antioch, writing early in the second century, criticized those who "allow not that the eucharist is the flesh of our Saviour Jesus Christ, which suffered for our sins, and which the Father of His goodness raised up."[17] For much of the first millennium, however, most Christians felt no pressing burden to define exactly what they meant when they repeated the words, "This is my body" and "This is my blood." A variety of orthodox opinion existed.

A ninth-century disputation between two monks from the Benedictine abbey at Corbie (France), Paschasius and Ratramnus, began to change the situation, although even their debate was more like a theological argument among colleagues than a sharp controversy. In his treatise on the Eucharist, Paschasius Radbertus, the abbot, insisted that, through consecration, the bread and wine of the Eucharist became Christ's body and blood in the physical sense and that Christians were bound to believe this doctrine.[18] In his response, Ratramnus, a theologian, insisted that the faithful receive the Lord's body and blood in symbol and that the physical body of Christ is not on the altar.[19] He insisted that the priest's consecration makes the bread and wine into a sacramental reality and that when Christians speak of Christ's body and blood they are using metaphorical language.[20] Here we find two strikingly different perspectives in dialogue with each other, but apparently without dire consequences to either person. They coexisted in the life of the Corbie monastery, and presumably they remained in Communion with each other. Paschasius' text, however, became the standard treatment of the subject.

The two centuries after the exchange of Paschasius and Radbertus were times of upheaval and unrest in western Europe. According to Gary Macy,

> Theologians had little time to think or write about the Lord's Supper (or anything else for that matter). When they did, however, they tended to read Paschasius, and slowly the theology of the abbot of Corbie became the standard way of thinking about the Eucharist.[21]

Thus, when Berengar of Tours revived the sacramental teachings of Ratramnus during the eleventh century, controversy ensued. The debate led to some unfortunate liturgical consequences. Following Ratramnus, Berengar insisted that the change in the bread and wine was a sacramental change, not a physical one. He was not rejecting the sacraments; rather, he was insisting that sacraments be understood sacramentally, that is, as signs that pointed to a spiritual reality and as symbols that actually participated in that reality. If the body and blood of Christ were literally present on the altar, not to mention in the mouths of the faithful, then the Eucharist was no longer a sacrament. That the body born of Mary could be physically on the altar was not only impossible, it was grotesque.[22]

The church could not, however, support such theological distinctions, and in 1059 Berengar was forced to recant his position and deliver the following oath:

> I, Berengar, an unworthy deacon of the Church of St. Maurice of Angers, acknowledging the true Catholic and Apostolic faith, anathematise every heresy, especially that concerning which I have hitherto been in ill repute, which attempts to affirm that the bread and wine which are placed on the altar are after consecration only a Sacrament and not the real body and blood of our Lord Jesus Christ, and that these cannot be held or broken by the hands of the priests or crushed by the teeth of the faithful with the senses but only by way of sacrament. . . . And I assent to the Holy Roman and Apostolic See, and with mouth and heart I profess that concerning the Sacrament of the Lord's Table I hold the faith which the Lord and venerable Pope Nicholas . . . and this holy synod have by evangelical and apostolic authority delivered to be held and have confirmed to me, namely that the bread and wine which are placed on the altar are after consecration not only a Sacrament but also the real body and blood of our Lord Jesus Christ, and with the senses . . . not only by way of Sacrament but in reality . . . these are held and broken by the hands of the priests and are crushed by the teeth of the faithful.[23]

Berengar's oath represents theology with all the subtlety of a bulldozer. Or, as Gary Macy wrote, it "is perhaps one of the most unfortunate and theologically inept statements ever put forward by the church on the subject of the Eucharist."[24] Macy further contends that, in spite of the oath, the best Catholic theologians began to undermine it almost immediately.[25] Indeed, Thomas Aquinas' definition of transubstantiation, in which the substance of the bread and wine changes, but not the accidents, stands against the shocking realism of Berengar's oath. Nevertheless, the sacramental realism represented by the oath had a profound effect on Catholic piety and liturgical practice. When the church faced the challenge of the Cathars, a dualistic and spiritualistic movement that challenged all practice of the sacraments, the Cathari cited Berengar's argument against the church.[26] Positions about the nature of the Eucharist hardened. It is significant that these controversies arose during a period of time when lay Communion was rare; most laymen and laywomen received Communion but once a year, on Easter.[27] In today's milieu, devotion to the Eucharist is demonstrated primarily through frequent reception, but the practice of frequent Communion was rare in the late Middle Ages, even though a devout Christian might go to mass regularly, even daily. Even among these regular worshipers, frequent Communion was considered presumptuous.[28]

Devotion to the Eucharist was shown in other ways. The consecrated host came to be treated as a relic.[29] Within the mass itself, the consecrated host was elevated after the priest said the Words of Institution. Sanctus bells would alert worshipers to look up, and the more enthusiastic among them might loudly exhort the priest to lift it higher. These worshipers were practicing an "ocular Communion," with grace of the sacrament received through seeing. Under that theology, the elevation was the high point of the mass. While these practices emerged primarily within the mass itself, under the pressure of the sacramental controversies, they spun off into independent devotional practices such as "benediction of the blessed sacrament," in which the reserved host was displayed before the people in a vessel known as a *monstrance* while the congregation offered hymns and prayers to the Christ believed present in that host. The development of these practices was in a sense a theological extension of the sacrament. Emblematic of this liturgical and devotional development was the emergence of the Feast of *Corpus Christi* (the Body of Christ) in response to pressures from the Cathari and other similar enthusiasts.[30] It was added to the Roman calendar in 1317, but it had been practiced since the previous century.[31] The feast was characterized by an exuberant public procession of the reserved sacrament. Although Palm Sunday processions of the reserved sacrament had been practiced in England as early as the eleventh century,[32] *Corpus Christi* was unique in that the entire feast was developed as a devotion to the reserved sacrament. Public sacramental processions for *viaticum* also emerged during the thirteenth century.[33] Of course, Christians had been delivering *viaticum* to the dying for centuries, but at one time it had been done discreetly, even secretly, in cloth bags or small boxes and other containers. During the late medieval period, it was done with processional cross, candles, incense, and vested clergy. These processions were, among other things, a public reminder of the church's commitment to eucharistic realism, and observing them became something of a badge of Catholic loyalty. These practices also became a target of criticism for the Protestant reformers of the sixteenth century.

Critique and Correction from the Reformers

Martin Luther insisted that practices of reservation and adoration developed because Catholics had neglected the most important point of all: Christ commanded his followers to eat the sacramental bread and drink the sacramental wine in remembrance of him. As we know, *viaticum* began in an attempt to heed that very commandment, but the reservation that eventually developed along with it presented different theological problems, especially when many Christians had separated the receiving of Communion from the mass itself. Luther's response was to reject much within late medieval eucharistic practice, including references to the Eucharist as a sacrifice. He insisted that proper eucharistic practice involved a pastor and congregation gathered together in obedience to Christ's commandment, with all receiving Communion in both the bread and the wine. In such a practice, reservation was unnecessary; and, as reservation ended, so would adoration of the sacrament. Thomas Cranmer and the English reformers followed a similar pathway. Although they retained more of the sacrificial language than Luther did, they radically reframed their understanding of it. In Cranmer's language, the Lord's Supper was not a sacrifice for sins past or present; that sacrifice had been accomplished on the cross once for all time. The Eucharist was "a sacrifice of praise and thanksgiving"[34] done in memory of Christ. *The Book of Common Prayer* insisted that worshipers were not worthy to offer any sacrifice to God, although they asked God to accept their sacrifice of praise and thanksgiving and grant them forgiveness of sins. In accordance with Luther's critique of Roman practice, Communion was given in "both kinds," that is, in both the bread and the cup.[35] Subsequently, Article XXX of the Anglican Articles of Religion, "Of Both Kinds," would reinforce this idea. It insisted, "The Cup of the Lord is not to be denied to the Lay-people; for both the parts of the Lord's Sacrament, by Christ's ordinance and commandment, ought to be ministered to all Christian men alike."[36]

Rubrics in the various editions of *The Book of Common Prayer* (or *BCP*) encouraged and enforced a movement away from reservation and related devotions. The 1549 *Book of Common Prayer*, often considered a conservative revision, allowed a limited practice of reservation. If a sick person were unable to come to the congregational service (called "the open communion"), at that service the priest could reserve "so much of the sacrament of the body and blood as shall serve the sick person, and so many as shall communicate with him . . ." He was to take the communion to them "so soon as he conveniently may, after the open communion ended in the church." The rubric does not allow for a general reservation; it was done only upon direct request to the priest, nor did it allow for reservation within the church itself.[37] The 1549 *BCP* also allowed for the priest with multiple sick calls to fulfill to offer a prayer of consecration in the home of the first parishioner visited and then give Communion at his subsequent stops without offering a new prayer of consecration.

> And if there be more sick persons to be visited the same day that the curate doth celebrate in any sick man's house; then shall the curate (there) reserve so much of the sacrament of the body and blood: as shall serve the other sick persons, and such as be appointed to communicate with them (if there be any). And shall immediately carry it, and minister it unto them.[38]

That provision was dropped from subsequent versions of the *BCP*. It is the last positive reference to reservation found in the English versions of the prayerbook, as well as the last action resembling what we now call extension of the table to the unwillingly absent.

The concluding rubric in the 1549 service for Holy Communion called for communicants to receive the elements "in their mouths, at the priest's hand," a practice that continued that of the Catholic Church. Why was this practice continued? While the rubric says that no commandment of Christ forbids receiving in the hand, receiving it in the mouth prevented people from taking the host away from the service and using it for "superstitious" and "wicked" uses,[39] that is, for amulets and charms. The fact that the rubric was included means that such practices probably still existed, although the rubric about receiving in the mouth was deleted from the 1552 *BCP*[40] and was not reintroduced in subsequent versions. The 1552 book did include the "black rubric,"[41] which further discouraged impulses toward adoration of the consecrated host. It said,

> Although no order can be so perfectly devised, but it may be of some, either for their ignorance and infirmity, or else of malice and obstinacy, misconstrued, depraved and interpreted in a wrong part: And yet because brotherly charity willeth, that so much as conveniently may be, offences should be taken away: therefore we willing do the same. Whereas it is ordained in the Book of Common Prayer, in the administration of the Lord's Supper,

that the Communicants kneeling should receive the holy Communion, which thing being well meant, for a signification of the humble and grateful acknowledging of the benefits of Christ, given unto the worthy receiver, and to avoid the profanation and disorder which about the holy Communion might else ensue: Lest yet the same kneeling might be thought or taken otherwise, we do declare that is not meant thereby, that any adoration is done, or ought to be done, either unto the Sacramental bread or wine there bodily received, or unto any real and essential presence there being of Christ's natural flesh and blood. For concerning the Sacramental bread and wine, they remain still in their very natural substances, and therefore may not be adored, for that were idolatry to be abhorred of all faithful Christians. And as concerning the natural body and blood of our savior Christ, they are in heaven and not here. For it is against the truth of Christ's true natural body, to be in more places than in one, at one time.[42]

There would be no adoration or actions perceived as such. Of course, perceptions are virtually impossible to regulate, and warnings against them suggest that the practice continued. The English reformers worked to make the service more like the holy meal of the community gathered around "God's board" and less like a sacrifice performed at a distant altar.

Equally significant is the rubric about the character of the bread itself. While the 1549 *BCP* had continued the use of wafer-like bread, a species that was more easily reserved, the rubric in the 1552 *BCP* called for use of more typical household bread. It said,

And to take away the superstition, which any person hath, or might have in the bread and wine, it shall suffice that bread be such, as is usual to be eaten at the Table with other meats, but the best and purest wheat bread, that conveniently may be gotten. And if any of the bread or wine remain, the Curate shall have it to his own use.[43]

The same rubric was repeated in the 1559 prayerbook.[44] It was altered for the 1662 *BCP*, the version of the prayerbook that was in use during John Wesley's lifetime. In that 1662 text, the rubric allows the curate to take home any unconsecrated bread and wine, but it directs that if any consecrated bread and wine remain at the close of the service,

It shall not be carried out of the Church, but the Priest, and such other of the Communicants as he shall then call unto him, shall, immediately after the Blessing, reverently eat and drink the same.[45]

In other words, remaining elements were not to leave the church but were to be reverently consumed by the faithful. These rubrics worked against any reservation of Holy Communion, ensuring that the Eucharist would be a service of the priest in the midst of his congregation and that there would be no devotional or pastoral extensions of the sacrament. None of the bread or wine would remain in the church, and none would be taken to the unwillingly absent.

What then could a priest of the Church of England do to provide Communion for the sick and dying members of a congregation? As noted, the 1549 *BCP* strictly limited reservation, and, beginning with the 1552 book, it was not permitted at all. There was no provision for clinical Communion (that is, Communion for the sick) or *viaticum* as an extension of the congregational service. Their prohibition represented a significant departure from Catholic tradition. The rubrics of the 1549 through 1662 prayerbooks insisted that the best preparation for sudden death was the frequent reception of Communion within the regularly appointed church services. If parishioners do that, they were told, "they shall have no cause in their sudden visitation to be unquieted for lacks of the same."[46] According to the rubric, there was no absolute right to *viaticum*; indeed, it was discouraged. Congregational Communion remained the norm.

In the event of sickness, congregants could arrange for a priest to come to the home and lead a service of Communion. Even in that case, the rubrics insisted that the priest maintain the standards of the Reformation. They insisted on the observance of a full service and the presence of a representative congregation. The 1552, 1559, and 1662 prayerbooks allowed for a priest to lead a Communion service for a solitary congregant only "in time of plague, sweat, or such other like contagious times of sickness or diseases, when none of the parish or neighbors can be gotten to communicate with the sick in their houses, for fear of infection."[47] In other circumstances, the communicant was expected to gather a congregation, and it appears that the priest could refuse the request when that was not accomplished. Thus, people could be given Communion in their homes, but even there the church maintained the ideal of the congregational service with the priest presiding. Ratification of the Articles of Religion (in 1571) further solidified the changes. Article XXVIII, "Of the Lord's Supper," outlawed reservation of the sacrament and processions of all kinds along with other devotions related to the consecrated host. It insisted, "The Sacrament of the Lord's Supper was not by Christ's ordinance reserved, carried about, lifted up, or worshipped."[48] Such was the tradition that John Wesley inherited.

John Wesley often served Communion to sick people and those who were dying, presumably doing so within the rubrics of the Church of

England described in the previous paragraphs. For example, after apparently spending the evening at a Fetter Lane love feast, Wesley made the following diary entry for 3 am(!), Monday, February 5, 1739: "At Mr. Thornbury's, Communion." He recorded a similar entry for that afternoon: "With Mrs. Preston, etc., religious talk, Communion, prayed." The "etc." refers to persons other than Wesley and the person named.[49] So it appears that a representative congregation had gathered.

His *Journal* entry for Wednesday, April 2, 1766, describes a Communion visit to a sick person along with the saving effect that the sacrament had on one of the other communicants. Thus, they fulfilled the rubric against solitary Communion while also demonstrating the power of the Lord's Supper as a converting ordinance. Wesley wrote,

> I visited a poor woman, who had been ill eight years, and is not yet weary or faint in her mind. An heavy-laden sinner desired to receive the sacrament with her, and found rest to her soul; and from that hour, increased every day in the knowledge and love of God.[50]

The impulse to offer *viaticum* remained. For instance, his entry for January 10, 1763, appears to be a reference to Communion with the dying: "I rode to Shoreham, and paid the last office of love to Mrs. Perronet."[51] A long entry dated September 3, 1782, provides another witness of a deathbed Communion. The haste with which Wesley moved to the appointment challenges the assertion that Communion for the dying was believed unnecessary:

> I preached in the street at Camelford. Being informed here, that my old friend Mr. Thompson, rector of St. Gennis, was near death, and had expressed a particular desire to see me, I judged no time was to be lost. So, borrowing the best horse I could find, I set out, and rode as fast as I could . . . . I found Mr. Thompson just alive, but quite sensible. It seemed to me as if none in the house but himself was very glad to see me. He had many doubts concerning his final state, and rather feared, than desired, to die; so that my whole business was to comfort him, and to increase and confirm his confidence to God. He desired me to administer the Lord's Supper, which I willingly did; and I left him much happier than I found him, calmly waiting till his change should come.[52]

Viaticum was offered, but not done from a reserved sacrament. Wesley offered "The Lord's Supper," that is, presumably the full prayerbook liturgy.

The order that Wesley provided in *The Sunday Service of the Methodists in America* follows that of *The Book of Common Prayer* (1662), although he omitted the rubric that refers to the plague along with the consolatory explanation given for those who "either by reason of extremity of sickness, or for want of warning in due time to the Curate, or for lack of company to receive with him, or by any other just impediment, do not receive the Sacrament of Christ's body and blood." Ironically, that line beginning with "the Curate shall instruct" is addressed, apparently, to the person who has missed *viaticum*,[53] which raises the question as to whether one can instruct a person who has missed *viaticum*. Perhaps Wesley saw the irony of the rubric and omitted it. *The Sunday Service* order for "The Communion of the Sick" includes the collect, Epistle (Hebrews 12:5-6), and Gospel (John 5:24) provided in the *BCP* followed by this rubric which refers one back to the standard order for the Lord's Supper: "After which the Elder shall proceed according to the form before prescribed for the Holy Communion, beginning at these words [Ye that do truly, & c.]."[54] A final rubric, which also follows the lead of the *BCP*, gives instructions on distribution of the elements. It called for the elder to receive first, as always, followed by other communicants, with Communion given "last of all to the sick person."[55] In summary, Wesley's order provided for a short service of the Word (a collect and the reading of three verses of scripture) along with the following from the order for the Lord's Supper:

> Invitation ("Ye that do truly . . .")
> Confession
> Comfortable Words
> *Sursum Corda* and Preface through the *Sanctus*
> Prayer of Humble Access
> Prayer of Consecration[56]

Distribution followed the prayer of consecration. One might presume some sort of closing prayer (perhaps extemporaneous) and a benediction, although Wesley's text does not mention anything after the distribution. As with the *BCP*, Wesley's order calls for the gathering of a representative congregation in the sick person's home. Thus, he envisioned a corporate service of the Lord's Supper, including ordained elder and a representative congregation, with a full prayer of consecration. The *Sunday Service* order was not an extension of the congregational Lord's Day Eucharist.

With the exception of the rubrics about the gathering of a congregation, Episcopal Methodism in America followed a variant of this practice through the publication of the aforementioned *United Methodist Book of Worship* (1992). The ritual presented in the first three hymnals of the twentieth century (1905, 1939, 1966) provides no separate service for the Communion of the sick, addressing the need, rather, within the rubrics that govern shortening of the full service when faced with time constraints. The 1905 rubric is typical:

> The Minister is expected to use the full form, but, if straightened for time in the usual administration of the Holy Communion, he may omit any part of the service, except the Invitation, the Confession, and the Prayer of Consecration; and in its administration to the sick he may omit any part of the service except the Confession, the Prayer of Consecration, and the usual sentences in delivering the Bread and Wine, closing with the Lord's Prayer, extemporary supplication, and the Benediction.[57]

The 1939 text omits reference to the Lord's Prayer as well as the extemporaneous prayer,[58] while the 1966 text insists that the shortened forms include both "the Prayer of Humble Access" and "the Prayer of Thanksgiving," that is, the post-Communion prayer of oblation ("O Lord, our heavenly Father, we thy humble servants, desire thy fatherly goodness mercifully to accept this our sacrifice of praise and thanksgiving . . .").[59]

The Book of Worship for Church and Home (1944) provides "An Order for the Administration of the Sacrament of the Lord's Supper or Holy Communion for the Sick and Others Confined to Their Homes." It replaces that traditional "Ye that do truly and earnestly repent . . ." invitation with scripture sentences and paraphrases drawn from Revelation 3:20, John 14:24, and 2 Corinthians 1:3-4. After that invitation, however, it follows a traditional Anglican-Methodist order: Confession, Prayer of Consecration, Prayer of Humble Access, Lord's Prayer, distribution, Prayer of Oblation, and benediction.[60] The 1964 *Book of Worship* offers no separate Communion service for the sick and homebound.

In summary, with the exception of the *Gloria in Excelsis*, which Wesley (following Cranmer) had placed at the end of the Service of the Lord's Supper, the 1966 Methodist rubrics for Communion of the sick followed Wesley's rubrics from 1784. An ordained or licensed minister led Communion for the sick, although, again, the rubrics that required the gathering of a congregation were no longer included in the ritual.

Restoration of an Ancient Practice and a Cautionary Word

It is clear, then, that the rubric printed in *The United Methodist Book of Worship* (1992), "A Service of Word and Table V with Persons Who Are Sick or Homebound," presented a major ritual change for the church:

> The pastor, or laypersons at the direction of the pastor, may distribute the consecrated bread and cup to sick or homebound persons as soon as feasible

following a service of Word and Table as an extension of that service. When this service is used as a distribution of the consecrated bread and cup, the Great Thanksgiving is omitted, but thanks should be given after the bread and cup are received.[61]

In many ways, the ritual text is similar to that provided in the 1662 *Book of Common Prayer*, Wesley's *Sunday Service*, and the various American Methodist rubrics noted above. It moves from invitation through confession, Communion, and benediction. The encouragement of lay administration and omission (or alteration) of the Great Thanksgiving, however, radically changes the dynamic of the service, making it possible to have an extension of the Sunday service and not simply a new Eucharist in an extended location. In essence, the church has moved past John Wesley and the arguments of the reformers and has returned to the second-century practice described by Justin Martyr in *First Apology*. I endorse the move for a variety of theological, liturgical, and pastoral reasons, which I will continue to outline in the remainder of this book. Employing laypersons to extend the congregational Eucharist ritualizes our common baptismal responsibility to maintain *koinonia* within the Body of Christ.

Nevertheless, a cautionary word is in order. The concern that led the reformers to craft rubrics against private Communions and against reservation of the sacrament arose from good intentions. Holy Communion is a corporate event that involves the entire community giving thanks and eating together. That connection is best preserved when thanksgiving, including acts of consecration, is done within the Lord's Day assembly and is immediately followed by the sacramental eating and drinking of the congregation. Hence comes the cautionary word about extending the table beyond the gathered congregation: Is there any danger, given the even small break between the eucharistic prayer and Communion that happens in ministries of the extended table, that United Methodists and others engaging in these ministries will eventually develop adoration practices akin to those that emerged in the medieval West during the eleventh century and later? In spite of our best intentions embodied in well-written rubrics about delivering the elements "as soon as feasible following a service of Word and Table,"[62] I have discovered that extending the table almost inevitably leads to some form of reservation, even if the elements are only stored temporarily in the sacristy refrigerator, in a chaplain's office, or in the home of a busy layperson who is willing to make the Communion visit but cannot do so immediately following the Sunday service. Furthermore, I am convinced that a full generation's use of a strong epiclesis with accompanying gestures in our Great Thanksgiving has made United Methodists more willing to believe that the elements do, indeed, become "the body and blood of Christ."[63] If the Spirit makes them so on Sunday morning, do they not remain so on Monday afternoon?

Will such modest reservation of the consecrated elements and increased use of classical epicletic sacramental language and ritual gestures lead mainline Protestants into practices of adoration? Lutheran liturgical historian and theologian Maxwell Johnson suggests that members of his denomination (The Evangelical Lutheran Church of America, or ELCA) might intentionally practice reservation for the sick and that such practices will not necessarily lead them back to benediction of the Blessed Sacrament and *Corpus Christi* processions. As he argues, when those late medieval practices emerged, they did so during a time of infrequent lay Communion, and so the various manifestations of ocular Communion emerged as a kind of spiritual compensation.[64] Since we now have a piety of frequent reception—not to mention, essentially no practice of non-communing attendance at the Eucharist—he insists that there is no danger of Protestants developing a theology and practice of ocular Communion. "The Lutheran Reformers," he argues, "were adamant that such 'food' was not an object to be adored *outside* of the overall liturgical *actio* but as a gift to be received within that *actio* ('Eucharist as meal') itself."[65] Within their contemporary theology he insists that there could be a Lutheran practice of reserving the sacrament for the sick and for emergencies that would not lead to the potentially troublesome practices of the late Middle Ages. Although Johnson does not apply his arguments to United Methodists, most of his historical and theological arguments regarding the ELCA can be extended to them as well.

Even with Johnson's argument, I am convinced that contemporary Christians cannot simply unwrite the history of *Corpus Christi* and its developments. Nor can we assume that the praxis of ocular Communion is dead. Those devotions continue on the popular level even if most liturgical scholars have little to do with them. Indeed, most United Methodist congregations include former Catholics, many of whom joined the UMC for reasons that do not include a rejection of their former piety. Plus, we have Episcopalians of an Anglo-Catholic piety who occasionally worship with us. If we begin reserving the sacrament for the sick, may we not assume that persons in United Methodist settings would begin practicing gestures of adoration, if nothing more than offering a modest bow when passing the Methodist "Tabernacle" or whatever we might decide to call our cabinet for storing the sacrament? Furthermore, for the sake of our sisters and brothers in other communions, should we not observe some minimal act of reverence? Moreover, further living into our now strong epiclesis might cause some of us to be troubled by our indifference to the presence of the consecrated elements, especially if we keep referring to them as "the body and blood of Christ." Given a practice of reservation, however modest it may be, are we so naïve that we think that practices of sincere reverence will not develop around it? Indeed, more than a few contemporary United Methodists bow toward the altar, even when there is no bread or wine on it. As we move deeper into eucharistic piety, we borrow gestures from those who have made this journey ahead of us.

Given such devotional realities within the contemporary ecumenical context, United Methodists must, therefore, write clear, well-founded rubrics as we begin to move more deeply into practices of the extended table. We need to state our intentions well at this early stage of the process. What should, and should not, be done with the elements set aside for extended table? How shall they be handled in the time between consecration and administration, especially if Communion is not held on the same day as consecration? I will say more about this matter in later chapters.

For now, given the sometimes-confusing *praxis* of ordination and eucharistic presidency within the United Methodist Church, in the next chapter I will address the relationship of those issues to the extension of Holy Communion.

Questions for Discussion

Have you been present for a Communion service celebrated in a hospital or home or in some other setting beyond the congregation? Describe the experience.

Describe the practice of extended table witnessed in *First Apology* by Justin Martyr. As you understand it, what pastoral and theological values were embodied in this practice? How do you assess those values?

In similar fashion, what pastoral and theological values were embodied in the various practices of reservation and adoration described in this chapter? How do you assess those values? What surprised you about these practices? What remaining questions do you have about them?

Describe the motivations that led the Protestant reformers to restrict private home Communion services.

Describe John Wesley's practice of serving Communion in private homes. As you see it, what spiritual and theological values were at work in his practice?

Is *viaticum* important? Why so?

Notes

1. *The United Methodist Book of Worship* (Nashville: The United Methodist Publishing House, 1992), 51-53.
   The Book of Discipline of the United Methodist Church, 1992 (Nashville: The United Methodist Publishing House, 1992), ¶ 1213.3.
2. From *The Book of Discipline of the United Methodist Church, 1996*, ¶ 331.1.b. Copyright © 1996 by the United Methodist Publishing House. Used by permission.
3. From *The Book of Discipline of the United Methodist Church, 2004*, ¶ 340.2.a.5. Copyright © 2004 by the United Methodist Publishing House. Used by permission.
4. *The First Apology of Justin Martyr* in *The Ante-Nicene Fathers, Translations of the Writings of the Fathers down to A.D. 325*. Eds. Alexander Roberts and James Donaldson. American reprint of the Edinburgh Edition, revised and chronologically arranged, with brief prefaces and occasional notes, by A. Cleveland Coxe, Volume I (Grand Rapids, Michigan: William B. Eerdmans Publishing Company, n.d.), chapter 67, 186.
5. Ibid.
6. "This Holy Mystery, A United Methodist Understanding of Holy Communion," *The Book of Resolutions of the United Methodist Church*, 2004 (Nashville: The United Methodist Publishing House, 2004), page 910.
7. Ibid., 923.
8. See, for instance, "Shifting Scholarly Perspectives" (pp. 1-20) and "Ancient Church Orders: A Continuing Enigma" (pp. 73-97) in Paul Bradshaw, *The Search for the Origins of Christian Worship, Sources and Methods for the Study of Early Liturgy*, second edition (Oxford: Oxford University Press, 2002).
9. *The Treatise of the Apostolic Tradition of St. Hippolytus of Rome*, edited by Gregory Dix and Henry Chadwick (London: The Alban Press, 1937), 58.
10. Ibid., 59.
11. Nathan Mitchell, *Cult and Controversy: The Worship of the Eucharist Outside Mass* (Collegeville, Minnesota: The Liturgical Press, 1982, 1990), 10-16.
12. Paul Bradshaw, *The Search for the Origins of Christian Worship, Sources and Methods for the Study of Early Liturgy*, second edition (Oxford: Oxford University Press, 2002), 82-3.
13. Nathan Mitchell, *Cult and Controversy*, 13-14.

14. W. H. (William Herbert) Freestone, *The Sacrament Reserved, A Survey of the Practice of Reserving the Eucharist, with Special Reference to the Communion of the Sick, During the First Twelve Centuries,* Alcuin Club Collection XXI (London: A. R. Mowbray and Company, Ltd.; Milwaukee, USA: The Young Churchman Company, 1917), 16-17.

15. See discussion in W. H. Freestone, *The Sacrament Reserved,* 58.

16. Ibid., 209.

17. Ignatius of Antioch, "To the Smyrnaeans," 6, in *The Apostolic Fathers, Comprising The Epistles (genuine and spurious) of Clement of Rome, The Epistles of S. Ignatius, The Epistle of S. Polycarp, The Martyrdom of S. Polycarp, The Teaching of the Apostles, The Epistle of Barnabas, The Shepherd of Hermas, The Epistle to Diognetus, The Fragments of Papias, The Reliques of The Elders Preserved in Irenaeus,* revised texts with short introductions and English translations, by the late J. B. Lightfoot, D.D., D.C.L., LL.D., Lord Bishop of Durham, Edited and Completed by J. R. Harmer, M.A., Fellow of Corpus Christi College, Cambridge, Sometime Chaplain to the Bishop. Published by the Trustees of the Lightfoot Fund (London and New York: Macmillan and Co., 1891), 158.

18. Paschasius of Corbie, *The Lord's Body and Blood,* translated by George E. McCracken and Allen Cabaniss, *Early Medieval Theology,* in *Library of Christian Classics,* IX (Philadelphia: The Westminster Press, 1957), 94.

19. Note discussion in Gary Macy, *The Banquet's Wisdom, A Short History of the Theologies of the Lord's Supper* (Akron, OH: OSL Publications, 2005), 88-89.

20. Ratramnus of Corbie, *Christ's Body and Blood,* Translated by George E. McCracken and Allen Cabaniss, *Early Medieval Theology,* in *Library of Christian Classics,* IX (Philadelphia: The Westminster Press, 1957), 193-94.

21. Gary Macy, *The Banquet's Wisdom,* 90. Reprinted by permission of OSL Publications.

22. Ibid., 90-99.

23. Berengarius, *Recantation* (1059), translated by Darwell Stone, *A History of the Doctrine of the Holy Eucharist* (London: Longmans, Green, and Company, 1909), I, 247.

24. Gary Macy, *The Banquet's Wisdom,* 94. Reprinted by permission of OSL Publications.

25. Ibid., 98.

26. Ibid., 102.

27. Eamon Duffy, *The Stripping of the Altars, Traditional Religion in England, 1400-1580* (New Haven: Yale University Press, 1992), 91-95.

28. Ibid., 93.

29. Nathan Mitchell, *Cult and Controversy,* 80-85, 116.

Of course, Christians had a long-standing practice of venerating the relics of saints, along with their graves.

30. Ibid., 172-73.

31. Christopher Walsh, "Corpus Christi," in *The New Westminster Dictionary of Liturgy and Worship,* Paul Bradshaw, ed. (Louisville: Westminster / John Knox Press, 2002), 136.

32. Nathan Mitchell, *Cult and Controversy*, 170-71.

33. Edward Foley, *From Age to Age, How Christians Have Celebrated the Eucharist* (Archdiocese of Chicago, 1991), 109.

34. "The Supper of the Lorde and the Holy Communion, Commonly Called the Masse," *The Book of Common Prayer* 1549. <http://justus.anglican.org/resources/bcp/1549/Communion_1549.htm>. Accessed November 17, 2006.

35. Ibid., accessed December 19, 2006.

36. Article XXX, "Of both kinds." <http://www.acl.asn.au/39articles.html#30>. Accessed November 9, 2006. The Articles of Religion were ratified in 1571.

Compare with the argument by Martin Luther in, "The Babylonian Captivity of the Church" Part I (1520) in *Martin Luther's Basic Theological Writings*, edited by Timothy F. Lull (Minneapolis: Fortress Press, 1989), 284-291.

37. "The Communion of the Sicke," *The Book of Common Prayer* 1549. <http://justus.anglican.org/resources/bcp/1549/Visitation_Sick_1549.htm #Communion>. Accessed December 19, 2006. I have, for the ease of the reader, updated the spelling in these references from the *BCP*. The original spellings can be viewed at the URL.

38. Ibid., Accessed November 17, 2006.

39. "Holy Communion," *The Book of Common Prayer* 1549. <http://justus.anglican.org/resources/bcp/1549/Communion_1549.htm>. Accessed November 10, 2006.

40. "The Order the Administracion of the Lordes Supper, or Holye Communion," *The Book of Common Prayer* 1552. <http://justus.anglican.org/resources/bcp/1552/Communion_1552.htm>. Accessed November 10, 2006.

41. Although its title may sound ominous to some, it was named "the black rubric," not for any strident or threatening tones, but rather for the color of the ink in which it was printed. It was a late addition to the text, and thus was printed in black instead of the standard red normally used for rubrics. Nevertheless, it was meant as a death knell for the medieval piety of reservation and adoration.

42. "Holy Communion," *The Book of Common Prayer* 1552. <http://justus.anglican.org/resources/bcp/1552/Communion_1552.htm>. Accessed November 10, 2006.

43. "Holy Communion," *The Book of Common Prayer* 1552. <http://justus.anglican.org/resources/bcp/1552/Communion_1552.htm>. Accessed November 10. 2006.

44. Ibid.

45. "The Order for the Administration of the Lord's Supper, or Holy Communion," *The Book of Common Prayer* 1662. <http://www.eskimo.com/ ~lhowell/bcp1662/communion/index.html>. Accessed November 10, 2006.

46. "The Communion of the Sicke," *The Book of Common Prayer* 1559. <http://justus.anglican.org/resources/bcp/1559/Visitation_Sick_1559.htm#Comm union>. Accessed December 27, 2007.

47. "The Communion of the Sicke," *The Book of Common Prayer* 1552. <http://justus.anglican.org/resources/bcp/1552/Visitation_Sick_1552.htm#Comm union>. Accessed December 27, 2007.

Note links to 1559 and 1662 books found on this same *Book of Common Prayer* website.

48. Article XXVIII, "Of the Lord's Supper," <http://www.acl.asn.au/39articles.html#28>. Accessed November 9, 2006.

49. Diary, February 5, 1739, *The Works of John Wesley*, Volume 19 *Journals and Diaries II (1738-1743)*, edited by W. Reginald Ward and Richard P. Heitzenrater (Nashville: Abingdon Press, 1990), 374.

50. Journal, April 2, 1766, *The Works of John Wesley*, Volume 3 (Grand Rapids, Michigan: Zondervan Publishing House, produced from an 1872 edition), 246.

51. Ibid., January 10, 1763, 125.

52. Journal, September 3, 1782, *The Works of John Wesley*, Volume 4 (Grand Rapids, Michigan: Zondervan Publishing House, produced from an 1872 edition), 235.

53. "The Communion of the Sick," *Book of Common Prayer*, 1662 (Cambridge University Press edition, 1968), 325.

54. *John Wesley's Prayer Book: The Sunday Service of the Methodists in North America*, with introduction, notes, and commentary by James F. White (Cleveland, Ohio: OSL Publications, 1991), 156. Reprinted by permission of OSL Publications.

55. Ibid.

56. *John Wesley's Prayer Book: The Sunday Service of the Methodists in North America*, with introduction, notes, and commentary by James F. White (Cleveland, Ohio: OSL Publications, 1991), 131-36.

57. *The Methodist Hymnal* (New York, Cincinnati: The Methodist Book Concern, 1905), 97 (The Ritual).

58. *The Methodist Hymnal* (Nashville and others: The Methodist Publishing House, 1939), 523.

59. *The Book of Hymns* (Nashville: Board of Publication of the Methodist Church, 1966), #830, 7-8, 17. Used by permission.

60. "An Order for the Administration of the Lord's Supper of Holy Communion for the Sick and Others Confined to Their Homes," *The Book of Worship for Church and Home* (Nashville: The Methodist Publishing House, 1944), 518-20.

61. *The United Methodist Book of Worship* (Nashville: The United Methodist Publishing House, 1992), 51. From "A Service of Word and Table V with Persons Who Are Sick or Homebound" ©1976, 1980 by Abingdon; ©1985, 1987, 1992 The United Methodist Publishing House. Used by permission.

62. Ibid.

63. Ibid., 38.

64. Maxwell E. Johnson, "Eucharistic Reservation and Lutheranism: An Extension of the Sunday Worship?" *Worship: Rites, Feasts, and Reflections* (Portland, Oregon: Pastoral Press, 2004), 159.

65. Ibid., 155. Used by permission.

3

"The Eye Cannot Say to the Hand . . ." Understanding the Role of the Clergy and the Laity

For many years, serving Communion was the exclusive domain of the clergy. As I mentioned earlier, when laypersons first began serving Communion within the Sunday liturgy, some were uncomfortable with the change, and others were suspicious of it. Was it proper for laypersons to serve Communion? Today, most congregations accept it as normal, but sometimes questions remain about laypersons serving Communion in homes. Is it acceptable, and, if so, under what conditions? I call this "The Big Question." Extended table Communion ministry will not happen if pastors and their congregations cannot answer it with a resounding "yes," along with an adequate rationale.

Of course my answer to "The Big Question" is "yes." Calling laypersons to take consecrated elements to the unwillingly absent is not functionally different from asking lay servers to carry Communion to people in the church balcony or nursery. When Communion servers drive several miles to the home of a shut-in church member, they are, in essence, extending the back wall of the sanctuary to them.[1]

What Do Elders Do at the Lord's Supper, and Why?

What do elders do at the Lord's Supper, and why? How does their work relate to the rest of the assembly? Many have perceived that relationship according to a hierarchical model of ministry.

I have seen this hierarchical model illustrated in the stones of a chapel that had once been part of a Catholic minor seminary.[2] As one walked up the center aisle of the nave toward the altar, one passed first the symbol for acolyte, then the symbol for lector, then, in succession, the symbols for sub-deacon, deacon, priest, and bishop. Here was illustrated a hierarchical ladder that one could ascend to the very top of ecclesiastical rank. Lest we believe that Catholics were the only ones who held such a hierarchical concept of ministry, we Methodists had once constructed a similar ladder. One became a member of the church through baptism, albeit a relatively powerless preparatory member. Confirmation brought one to full membership and admission to Communion. When ordained a deacon, one was given probationary membership in the Annual Conference and some limited authority to preside at the sacraments. Elders gained full conference membership and full sacramental rights. One might ascend the ladder even further, perhaps becoming a district superintendent or even a bishop. Some believed that denominational executives and even seminary professors lived near the top of the ladder as well.[3] When viewed according to this hierarchical model, consecrating the Eucharist was something that the clergy did for the rest of the church. That perspective was supported by an architecture that often placed the Communion altar on the front wall of the church—or, in the Akron Plan, directly in front of the pulpit with no space between them—and by a rubric that called for pastors to offer the Prayer of Consecration while "facing the Lord's Table."[4] They offered the prayer with their backs to the congregation, and when the work of consecration was done, they brought the elements down from the altar to the people.

Some assumptions based on this model of accumulating rank remain with us, but a more circular baptismal model based on 1 Corinthians 12 challenges them. Instead of the ministerial ladder, this alternative model, "the Body of Christ," places baptism at the center of church life with the various gifts and vocations radiating from that center.[5]

> For just as the body is one and has many members, and all the members of
> the body, though many, are one body, so it is with Christ. For in the one

Spirit we were all baptized into one body—Jews or Greeks, slaves or free—
and we were all made to drink of one Spirit (1 Corinthians 12: 12-13).

According to Paul's model, baptism is the foundational identity marker
for the Christian, and all partake of the one Spirit given there. Within the one
Body of Christ, baptismal identity is expressed in a variety of gifts and leadership roles, including, among others, those of "apostles . . . prophets . . .
(and) teachers," as well as "various kinds of leadership" (1 Corinthians 12:
28). All of these gifts and callings exist for the edification of the whole body,
and each is needed; none may despise another. Thus, "the eye cannot say to
the hand, 'I have no need of you,' nor again the head to the feet, 'I have no
need of you'" (1 Corinthians 12:21). This model of the Body of Christ has
been the foundational metaphor for the Liturgical Movement, and it takes the
shape of an altar-table surrounded on three sides by a congregation with the
pastor looking across the table at the gathered community. As one of the baptized, the elder fulfills his or her role in the midst of the gathered congregation, not apart from it. The gifts bestowed in and through baptism are
identified and nurtured by the community. At ordination, the church prays
that pastoral gifts may be further strengthened in grace and power.
Ordination loses no dignity under this understanding, but we raise the dignity of the other baptized Christians, along with our expectations of them.

Within this model, leadership of the Great Thanksgiving remains in the
hands of the pastor, and rightly so; but how do we understand this pastoral
work, especially in relation to extending Holy Communion to the unwillingly absent? First of all, to say that the clergyperson prays the Great
Thanksgiving by himself or herself misreads the classical liturgical tradition
that is expressed within the official services of the United Methodist Church
and other mainline denominations. It is better to say that she or he leads it
in concert with the gathered people of God. With its dialogical structure, the
Great Thanksgiving requires at least one person other than the pastor and
preferably a full congregation.[6] This structure reflects wisdom established in
the eucharistic reforms of the English Reformation, which forbade the practice of the solitary mass. As the following rubric from the 1559 *Book of
Common Prayer* stated:

> And there shall be no celebration of the lord's supper except there be a good
> number to Communicate with the priest, according to his discretion.
>
> And if there be not above twenty persons in the Parish of discretion to
> receive the communion, yet there shall be no communion, except four or
> three at the least, communicate with the priest . . .[7]

So, our tradition insists that a congregation must be present along with a pastor. The two principles work together.

Reserving leadership of the Great Thanksgiving to the clergy provides a safeguard which supports the most basic eucharistic ethic, the doctrine expressed by Paul in 1 Corinthians 11:

> For all who eat and drink without discerning the body, eat and drink judgment against themselves . . . . So then, my brothers and sisters, when you come together to eat, wait for one another (1 Corinthians 11: 29, 33).

Without such waiting and gathering, Paul insisted, their meal was "not really . . . the Lord's Supper" (1 Corinthians 11: 20). Simply reciting the correct prayer could not make it so. The best eucharistic rubrics, ancient and modern, are designed to safeguard and express unity within the Body of Christ. Clergy are not given a special ontological power for their ministry at the Lord's Table; rather they are given a special role and responsibility. Their role is to convene the church—if you will, to hold and administer "the keys of the kingdom" (Matthew 16:19). If they alone can lead their brothers and sisters in this prayer, then the congregation must assemble in order to offer its Eucharist; Christians must "wait for one another." In that light, ancient teaching about the special role of the clergy makes more sense, such as this classic text from the pen of St. Ignatius:

> Let that be held a valid eucharist which is under the bishop or one to whom he shall have committed it. Wheresoever the bishop shall appear, there let the people be; even as where Jesus may be, there is the universal Church. It is not lawful apart from the bishop either to baptize or to hold a love-feast; but whatsoever he shall approve, this is well-pleasing also to God . . . It is good to recognize God and the bishop . . . . he that doeth aught without the knowledge of the bishop rendereth service to the devil.[8]

Again, under such a discipline, the pastor is not permitted to celebrate the Eucharist by himself or herself, and groups of Christians cannot do so without their pastor. The ancient disciplines for carrying Communion to the unwillingly absent that we described in chapter two developed as an extension of that commitment to church unity.[9]

An elder, then, calls a congregation to gather, and then he or she leads the Great Thanksgiving in concert with them, each person fulfilling his or her particular role. I do not, by the way, endorse the practice of people in the congregation in turn voicing the words in the body of that prayer. Such a practice seeks to embody the egalitarian nature of the baptismal community, but it unwittingly undermines that vision. The practice of multiple voices reading the prayer implies that saying those words is the most important thing that one can do, that the pastoral role is, after all, the most significant. A similar problem is created when the Words of Institution and the epiclesis are reserved to the pastor while the remainder of the text is parceled out either to laypersons or to deacons. That practice implies a hierarchy within the text itself, with the ordained elder speaking the really important (magic?) words. Against this misshapen practice, I contend that the most important action in the Eucharist is not the presiding, but rather the receiving of Holy Communion and living more deeply into the *koinonia* that God offers there.

Before we leave this discussion of the elder's role, we need to assert that there is no absolute right to preside at the Lord's Table, even among elders. Presiding is done for the sake of the assembly and for no other reason. For instance, I am appointed to serve as a professor in a School of Theology, and thus I am not currently the pastor of a local congregation. I normally go to church on Sundays, and I receive Communion when it is offered, but I preside at the Lord's Table only when I am specifically asked to do so. Nor would it be proper for me to set up a competing Service of Word and Table, say, in my neighborhood. The *Discipline* forbids it,[10] not to mention the accepted standards of pastoral ethics. Although we have a substantial number of ordained faculty members and staff at Perkins School of Theology, even in that setting elders do not preside at will, but only when the chapel committee or the dean asks them to do so. The annual conference follows a similar discipline; elders abound, but the bishop and the annual conference worship committee extend invitations to preside. Properly understood, the right to preside always serves the church and its liturgical assembly, not vice versa. At the end of the day, it matters that the church celebrates the Eucharist, not which particular elder gets to preside.

I did not understand this dynamic very well until my time as a student in the Doctor of Theology program at Boston University. I returned to school full time after serving as a pastor of local congregations for eleven years, which at the time represented most of my adult life. Setting the pastoral role aside for a time was more painful that I might have imagined, and I grieved the change, but the grief brought me to a good place. I came to realize that the Eucharist was not about me, about what I needed to do as an elder. Thus, in addition to the academic work that I did at that time, my spiritual work involved developing an adult spirituality that was rooted in my baptism as much as it was rooted in my ordination. I am still working on this spiritual project, but I think that doing so has made my pastoral work better, both when I returned to the parish after my time at Boston and now in my work as a professor of worship at Perkins School of Theology.

What Do Laypersons Do at the Lord's Supper, and How Is That Work Extended?

Now we must move to our second question: What do laypersons do at the Lord's Supper, and how is that work extended beyond the assembly? In other words, what do laypersons do both within the liturgy itself and after they have been dismissed from it? Here is a summary of what happens at the Eucharist: (1) The church gathers, and it maintains and strengthens that gathering through confession, pardon, and reconciliation. (2) Together, the church offers a sacrifice of praise and thanksgiving, which includes epiclesis, or prayer for an effective sacrament. (3) Church members receive Communion, and they also serve it to each other. Although the ordained person leads the church through these three movements, when viewed in the broad sense none of them is specific to ordination. All members of the church participate in each, although they do so in different ways.

Each of the three movements is complex. For instance, a commitment to gathering requires conversations about transportation, parking, and meeting times, as well as physical accessibility. Can a person confined to a wheelchair find a reasonably close place to park, and can she then make her way from her car into the worship space without undue trouble? What about the hotel staff person who cleaned up after Saturday's wedding reception? Can he find a Sunday service that reasonably fits his schedule?[11] These are questions for the whole church to consider, as are continuing discussions about the appropriate shape of confession and reconciliation. What should confession look like in any particular local context?[12]

The commitment to receiving Communion—in both kinds, no less—is another complex question. It also calls for the removal of barriers. Again, in previous writing, I related this question both to the use of wine as an ecumenical sign and standard and to the use of grape juice as accommodation for alcoholics and as a witness to abstinence.[13] Negotiating this tension between norm and exception is a challenge for the whole church as is the similar problem presented by persons who suffer from Celiac Disease, an allergic condition that can be controlled only with total abstinence from wheat gluten.[14] How do persons living with Celiac Disease receive Communion under the sign of traditional bread? The doctrine of concomitance—the assertion that one receives the fullness of Christ's presence in either the sacramental bread or wine—has often been invoked as an answer to such dilemmas. Nevertheless, its connection to the withholding of the cup from the laity gives us pause. Our historic commitment to the both kinds doctrine, that is, to receiving Communion under the sign of both bread and wine, should cause us to consider providing an alternative, gluten-free form of bread for those who need it. Making such exceptions, however, can cause us to lose touch with the symbols of one loaf, one cup. Congregations need to wrestle with such questions.

The commitment to serve one another also invites our deeper reflection. Catholic liturgical scholar Robert Taft has argued that everyone in the assembly, including the pastor who speaks the Great Thanksgiving, should receive Communion from the hand of another. Taft wrote,

> The general rule in communion rites right up through the Middle Ages, in both East and West, was that communion is not just *taken*, not even by the clergy, but *given* and *received*. For communion is at once a ministry and a gift and a sharing, and as such is *administered* to the communicant through the hands of another.[15]

According to this understanding, serving Communion is the work of the whole assembly. At the point of receiving, it is clear that the elder, although ordained, remains part of the *laos*, part of the whole people of God. Ordination is not graduation from the *laos*. The practice commended by Taft runs counter to longstanding Methodist practice as inherited from the Church of England. Normally, clergy served themselves. Indeed, the rubric in *The Book of Hymns* (1966) says, "The minister shall first receive the Holy Communion in both kinds, and then shall deliver the same to any who are assisting him."[16] That rubric is virtually the same as the one found in *The Book of Common Prayer* (1662).[17] We do well to adopt Taft's option.

Clearly, using laypersons to take Communion to the homes of the unwillingly absent does not circumvent the authority or proper role of the pastor. The work of taking Communion to the unwillingly absent is part of this commitment to serve Communion to each other. The commitment to serve one another invites our deeper reflection; it fulfills the church's purpose in coming to the Eucharist—to manifest the unity of the Body of Christ. Doing so means that carrying the elements into homes should be a clear extension of the Sunday service, as the work of Laurence Stookey has made clear.[18]

I have, then, offered a clear and positive rationale for using trained laypersons to carry Communion to shut-in and other unwillingly absent church members. In such a process, lay and clergy roles are both honored and fully exercised. In the next chapter, I will offer detailed directions for conducting such a Communion visit. However, before leaving the subject of proper roles, I will offer some reflection on the work of licensed local pastors, commissioned ministers, and deacons, as that work relates to extended Communion.

Licensed Local Pastors, Commissioned Ministers, and Deacons: How Do the Principles Apply?

To this point, I have described the work of elders as it relates to the ministry of the laity. I have insisted that each has a vital role to play in the celebration of the Lord's Supper. There are, of course, some people living within United Methodist polity who do not easily fit these categories of clergy and lay. Local pastors and commissioned ministers preparing for ministry as elders may receive a license to preside at the Lord's Table, but they may do so only within their specific pastoral appointments.[19] Some would assert that these people are neither fish nor fowl, neither clergy nor lay; sometimes it seems that they exist in an ecclesiastical limbo somewhere between the two. How do we understand their work, and how do the principles described earlier apply to their work?

Although elders, local pastors, and commissioned ministers do not have ordination to Word, Sacrament, and Order in common, they do, in fact, each receive the bishop's appointment. This commonality lends the system its ecclesiastical coherence. As I noted in the earlier discussion of elders, United Methodist polity appointment is a key consideration for sacramental ministry. On that matter, United Methodists have more in common with Catholics than they may realize. For instance, if a Catholic priest decides to marry, permission to preside at the Eucharist may be withdrawn, although Catholics understand that the ordination remains intact; episcopal appointment functions in tandem with ordination. The United Methodist system extends the principle expressed by Ignatius of Antioch (107 CE) that we discussed earlier: "Let that be held a valid eucharist which is under the bishop or one to whom he shall have committed it."[20] In that polity, the bishop is the primary minister of the sacraments, and all others preside by special permission. Ignatius makes no mention of presbyters, that is, of elders.

The United Methodist system is not inconsistent with the Ignatian precedent, with its claims about the prerogatives and responsibilities of bishops. Within local United Methodist congregations, then, what I have said about elders also applies to the work of local pastors who have been granted a license for pastoral ministry and of commissioned ministers on the elder track. Doubtless, some United Methodists would want to temper Ignatius' enthusiastic defense of episcopal prerogatives, but that is matter for another day.

Ordained deacons have a different role to fulfill, one that contemporary United Methodists are still working to understand and practice. Our current understanding of a diaconate that is distinct from the office of elder (presbyter) has deep historical roots,[21] but we have only been practicing it since 1996. Before that time, United Methodist ordination proceeded according to the ladder model described earlier, with ordination as elder following several years after one was ordained a deacon. The change in polity has caused some confusion. Like others who moved through the ordained ministry process before 1996, I am ordained both deacon (1981) and elder (1986). Ministry candidates who enter the process now must discern one path or the other.[22] I was appointed as a pastor of local congregations during my (first) five years as a deacon,[23] and thus I presided at our celebrations of the Lord's Supper; many others had a similar experience, and so some deacons under the current system have wondered why they are not able to do the same. In like manner, some superintendents have wondered why they cannot appoint deacons to care for the sacramental needs of congregations. Indeed, legislation passed at the 2008 General Conference says the following:

> For the sake of extending the mission and ministry of the church, a pastor-in-charge or district superintendent may request that the bishop grant local sacramental authority to the deacon to administer the sacraments in the absence of an elder within a deacon's primary appointment.[24]

How shall we receive this new provision? Strictly speaking, understand that I presided at Table only as one appointed by the bishop to serve as a pastor, and not intrinsically out of my role as a deacon. Indeed, I had served as a licensed local pastor for two years (1979-1981) before I was ordained as a deacon, and I presided at the Lord's Table during that time as well, again strictly within the limits of my appointment.

Note that the new policy is a missional exception, and it should remain just that, an exception that the bishop invokes in emergency circumstances. Outside of such circumstances, we should continue to presume classical, non-exceptional roles for elders, deacons, and laypersons. Even if United Methodist deacons may, at times, lead the Great Thanksgiving during extended table visits, we still want laypersons to hold a central role in the work of the extended table.

Although I served as a deacon for five years before I was ordained an elder, most of my colleagues and I functioned as something like "elders in training," and we were not encouraged to develop a diaconal identity. With the current system of complementary orders, we now have opportunity to regain the fullness of the diaconal role for the mission and witness of the church, and we need to give ourselves several generations to live into this new spiritual reality. According to the *Discipline*, "Deacons give leadership in the church's life . . . by assisting the elders in the administration of the sacraments of baptism and the Lord's Supper."[25] What is the proper shape of such assistance? As noted earlier, pastors are called "to select and train deacons and lay members to serve the consecrated Communion elements";[26] thus we may assume that deacons should make themselves available for such training and subsequent service. Beyond that, the *Discipline* does not say much about what such assisting of the elders might look like, and neither do the various services of Word and Table in *The United Methodist Hymnal* and *The United Methodist Book of Worship*.

The Services for the Ordering of Ministry in The United Methodist Church (also known as *The Ordinal*) do, however, provide such a model. The examination of deacons repeats the earlier assertions about assisting the elder and doing ministries of compassion. It says,

> A deacon is called . . . to assist elders at Holy Baptism and Holy Communion, . . . to serve all people, particularly the poor, the sick, and the oppressed, and to lead Christ's people in ministries of compassion and justice.[27]

Rubrics within *The Ordinal* Eucharist give some shape to this charge. A rubric before the Great Thanksgiving states, "Deacons prepare the table for the Lord's Supper"; it then refers the reader to the extended rubrics on page 26 of *The United Methodist Book of Worship*.[28] These rubrics in *The Book of Worship* describe the presentation of offerings, including the bread and cup, along with the uncovering and other preparations of the elements for the Great Thanksgiving.[29] According to *The Ordinal*, the deacon, presumably, may do all of this action. An *Ordinal* rubric under "Giving the Bread and Cup" directs that "the bread and cup (be) given to the people by new elders and new deacons" with other clergy and laity assisting them as necessary.[30] A further rubric says, "when all have received, the deacons put the Lord's Table in order."[31] Significantly, the rubrics in *The Ordinal* service also call for a deacon to participate in the dismissal. After the bishop blesses the people, "a newly ordained deacon" dismisses them, saying, "Go in peace to serve God and your neighbor in all that you do."[32] To summarize, in these rubrics we see a significant embodiment of the deacon's historic role, specifically the following:

1. Preparation of the table for Communion;
2. Serving Communion;
3. Putting the table in order after Communion;
4. Dismissing the people to their mission.

Traditionally, deacons have stood on the bridge between the church's liturgy and its mission; one might also think of them as standing in the doorway of the church, keeping mission and liturgy in active dialogue. Deacons receive offerings, and they distribute gifts within the assembly and also beyond its walls to the poor and others in need, including Communion of the unwillingly absent. By dismissing the congregation, they bid them join the mission that the deacons are leading. Within *The Ordinal*, the bishop leads the primary work of intercession as he or she prays for the ordinands. Within the regular Lord's Day worship of congregations, however, deacons have traditionally led the intercessions, which become another liturgical embodiment of the church's mission.

While the *Discipline* requires pastors to train deacons and laity for the work of serving the Communion elements,[33] we can now observe that much of the work involved with extended table Communion is diaconal in character. Packing Communion kits is a form of putting the table in order. Maintaining a home Communion list links liturgy and the mission of pastoral care. Sending home Communion servers to their visits is one aspect of the missional charge given to the entire congregation. Since these actions are clearly diaconal, then it would seem that deacons should also participate with pastors both in training home Communion servers and in administering the ongoing work of the home Communion team.

Since, however, most United Methodist congregations do not have a deacon, this discussion about the relationship of elders and deacons must remain an abstract one for many. Deacons tend to become something of an ecclesiastical luxury item, hired primarily by the congregations that can afford them. Congregations that do not enjoy the services of a deacon must find some other ways to fulfill the missional and pastoral functions that we have identified here. We believe that God will provide such means, but a fuller embodiment of ministry is witnessed when both a deacon and an elder/pastor are in residence within a congregation. Such fullness is not likely to occur, however, under the current polity, in which bishops have little effective control over the appointment of deacons. Political considerations aside, the ministry of the extended table offers a promising opportunity for the development of the United Methodist diaconate.

Questions and Topics for Discussion

Describe the roles of the ministers listed below as each relates to the Lord's Supper:

> Elders and other Pastors appointed to serve local congregations;
>
> Deacons;
>
> Laypersons, including home Communion servers.

How are their roles distinct? How do they relate to each other?

Why is it important that clergy preside at the Lord's Table? Why is it equally important that they not preside when there is no congregation present?

Why is it important that each person in the congregation receive Communion from another sister or brother in Christ? What is it like for you to receive Communion from someone else? What is it like for you to offer it to another?

A fellow church member challenges you, saying that because you are not ordained, it is not proper for you to make home Communion visits. How do you explain yourself?

Notes

1. Various insights in this chapter first appeared in the following article that I wrote: "Shall United Methodist Laypersons take Communion to the Unwillingly Absent?—Historical, Theological, and Pastoral Issues," *Sacramental Life* 8:3 (Ordinary Time 1995), 31-36. © Copyright The Order of Saint Luke. Article used by permission.

2. Minor seminaries are, essentially, high schools for prospective priests. Many of these institutions were closed as the Catholic Church looked for new models of vocational discernment.

3. This paragraph is drawn from my article "What is an Order? Reflections on the Vocation of Elders and Deacons." *Quarterly Review* 24:4 (Winter 2004), 340. Used by permission.

4. *The Book of Hymns, Official Hymnal of the United Methodist Church* (Nashville: The United Methodist Publishing House, 1966), 830, ritual page 15.

5. "What is an Order? Reflections on the Vocation of Elders and Deacons," *Quarterly Review* 24:4 (Winter 2004), 341. Used by permission.

6. See the rubrics in and dialogical pattern in "A Service of Word and Table I, "The *United Methodist Book of Worship* (Nashville: The United Methodist Publishing House, 1992), 36-38.

Note the following paragraphs in *The Book of Discipline of the United Methodist Church* (Nashville: The United Methodist Publishing House, 2004), ¶ 305, ¶ 340.2.a, ¶ 344.3, ¶ 1117.9.

7. *The Book of Common Prayer* 1559. <http://justus.anglican.org/resources/bcp/1559/Communion_1559.htm>. Accessed December 27, 2007.

The same rubric is found in the Communion Service of the 1662 *Book of Common Prayer.* <http://www.eskimo.com/~lhowell/bcp1662/communion/index.html>. Accessed November 29, 2006.

8. Ignatius of Antioch, "To the Smyrnaeans," 8-9, in *The Apostolic Fathers, Comprising The Epistles (genuine and spurious) of Clement of Rome, The Epistles of S. Ignatius, The Epistle of S. Polycarp, The Martyrdom of S. Polycarp, The Teaching of the Apostles, The Epistle of Barnabas, The Shepherd of Hermas, The Epistle to Diognetus, The Fragments of Papias, The Reliques of The Elders Preserved in Irenaeus*, revised texts with short introductions and English translations, by the late J. B. Lightfoot, D.D., D.C.L., LL.D., Lord Bishop of Durham, Edited and Completed by J. R. Harmer, M.A., Fellow of Corpus Christi College, Cambridge, Sometime Chaplain to the Bishop. Published by the Trustees of the Lightfoot Fund (London and New York: Macmillan and Co., 1891), 158.

9. See a similar discussion in my book *Sacraments and Discipleship, Understanding Baptism and the Lord's Supper in a United Methodist Context* (Nashville: Discipleship Resources, 2001), 92-95.

10. *The Book of Discipline of the United Methodist Church*, 2004 (Nashville: The United Methodist Publishing House, 2004), ¶ 341.4.

11. I am not saying that every United Methodist congregation must answer "yes" to this question, but given a connectional system, it is not unreasonable to expect that at least *one* United Methodist congregation in each reasonably sized city should be able to do so.

12. See the discussion of confession and reconciliation in my book, *Sacraments and Discipleship*, 78-85.

13. Mark W. Stamm, *Sacraments and Discipleship*, 104-05.

14. Wanda Zemler-Cizewski, "The Eucharist and the Consequences of Celiac Disease: A Question of Access to Holy Communion," *Worship* 74:3 (May 2000), 237-47.

15. Robert F. Taft, "Receiving Communion—A Forgotten Symbol?" *Beyond East and West, Problems in Liturgical Understanding* (Washington, D.C., The Pastoral Press, 1984), 102. Used by permission.

16. *The Book of Hymns* (Nashville: The Methodist Publishing House, 1966), 830, ritual page 17. Used by permission.

17. "The Order of the Administration of the Lord's Supper, or Holy Communion," *The Book of Common Prayer* 1662. <http://www.eskimo.com/~lhowell/bcp1662/communion/index.html>. Accessed December 6, 2006.

18. Laurence Hull Stookey, *Eucharist, Christ's Feast in the Church* (Nashville: Abingdon Press, 1993), 156.

19. *The Book of Discipline of the United Methodist Church* 2004, ¶ 315, ¶ 316, ¶ 326.2.

20. Ignatius of Antioch, "To the Smyrnaeans," 8-9, p. 158.

21. Acts 6:1-7.
The First Apology of Justin Martyr in *The Ante-Nicene Fathers, Translations of the Writings of the Fathers down to A.D. 325.* Eds. Alexander Roberts and James Donaldson. American reprint of the Edinburgh Edition, revised and chronologically arranged, with brief prefaces and occasional notes, by A. Cleveland Coxe, Volume I (Grand Rapids, Michigan: William B. Eerdmans Publishing Company, n.d.), chapter 67, 186.

22. *The Book of Discipline of the United Methodist Church*, 2004, footnote 3 to ¶ 311, pp. 203-05, especially points 5 and 8 on page 205.

23. I try to avoid speaking of my work as a deacon in the past tense, because my deacon's ordination remains. I might better refer to the time when I was *only* ordained as a deacon and was not yet an elder, but the grammatical structure seems awkward, and it is hard to differentiate between the two periods in my ordained life without making the diaconal ordination sound like a lesser state. Regardless, I remain deacon and elder. Nevertheless, I contend that the church never seriously worked at nurturing that dual identity, but rather has thought of me and my remaining deacon-elder colleagues simply as elders. They would think it strange were any of us to show up at a meeting of the Order of Deacons.
I am not, of course, looking for another meeting to attend.

24. *The Book of Discipline of the United Methodist Church*, 2008 (Nashville: The United Methodist Publishing House, 2008), ¶ 328.

25. *The Book of Discipline of the United Methodist Church-2004*, ¶ 328.

26. Ibid., ¶ 340.2.c.5.

27. *Services for the Ordering of Ministry in the United Methodist Church* (Prepared by The General Board of Discipleship and The General Board of Higher Education and Ministry in collaboration with The Council of Bishops, approved by the General Conference, 2004), 22-23. Revised from "The Order for the

Ordination of Deacons" from *The United Methodist Book of Worship* ©1992, The United Methodist Publishing House. Used by permission.

28. *Services for the Ordering of Ministry in the United Methodist Church*, 28.

29. *The United Methodist Book of Worship*, 26.

30. *Services for the Ordering of Ministry in the United Methodist Church*, 31.

31. Ibid.

32. Ibid., 32.

33. *The Book of Discipline of the United Methodist Church*, 2004, ¶ 340.2.c.5.

4

Conducting the Visit

We come now to a discussion of the Communion visit itself. This is the "how to do it" chapter on home Communion serving. In the previous chapters, we have covered sufficient historical and theological ground for you to understand the background of this practice, its importance in the ongoing life of the church, and the role you play as a home Communion server. Of course, all of us who minister at the Lord's Supper need to continue reading and reflecting about what we are doing there, and you are no exception. As you will see, other important questions will come to the fore as we walk through the steps involved in making Communion visits. Such is the nature of liturgical theology.

I have arranged this chapter as a dialogue with the text that I suggest you use when you lead these visits. Like all liturgical texts, this one contains the *ordinary* along with reference to the *propers*. It also contains *rubrics*. I will explain what I mean by each of these terms, and how each category functions. As we discuss the text, let us remember, however, that liturgies are ritual actions that people do together. Thus, the printed order of worship offered here is not the liturgy any more than a cookbook is a meal. A printed order is a guide to holding a liturgy. The liturgy is what people actually do when they gather, and it is always more than a simple reading of words, regardless of how good those words may be.

Rubrics

Because liturgies involve a combination of words and action, *rubrics*—the printed directions given to worship leaders and to the congregation—are vitally important. Such directions are called rubrics because historically they have often been written in red print. In *The United Methodist Hymnal* and *The United Methodist Book of Worship,* they are printed in red and also italicized. Thus, they are clearly distinguished from the parts of the service that are normally read aloud.[1] Here, they are simply italicized.

Rubrics are vitally important to the conduct of the liturgy, just as directions to "bring to a boil" or "bake for twenty minutes at four hundred degrees" are as important to the process of preparing food as are the ingredients and their proportions. In the text that follows, the rubrics are written in italics. Note them as you plan, and take them seriously. They provide important guidance.

The Ordinary

The *ordinary* is that part of the liturgy that remains the same each time it is used. Like the Lord's Day service that sends the servers to their visit, the liturgy recommended here also includes a Service of the Word and a Service or the Table. In this order, the opening prayer ("Almighty God, to you all hearts are open . . . etc.")[2] is part of the ordinary for the Service of the Word. So is the order of worship that includes Greeting, Act of Praise, scripture reading, and intercessory prayers. "A Service of Word and Table V, With Persons Who Are Sick of Homebound," drawn from *The United Methodist Book of Worship*, provides the ordinary for the service of the extended table and is used each time it is offered, perhaps with a Great Thanksgiving if a pastor is present, and if not, without.[3] The rubrics are also part of the ordinary, since they remain the same. Familiarity with the ordinary allows one to participate in a liturgy without undue preoccupation with what is coming next. Knowing the ordinary is like knowing the steps of a dance. Deep familiarity, even memorization, gives freedom.

The Propers

The *propers* are the adjustable or changeable parts of the liturgy, such as the scripture readings and hymns, and the specific prayers that you will offer. Indeed, the best liturgies are a healthy balance of ordinary and propers, of fixed and flexible parts. You will not find propers noted in the text offered below. Planning them is your task. You will be asked to provide a reading for the day and comments on it, an act of praise, and specific intercessory prayers. The rubrics will guide you in your planning and use of the propers. As with any liturgy, you may need to adjust your plans as the service unfolds. Ability to adjust is a function of good leadership in many realms, and here is no exception. But leadership, not to mention adjustments, becomes more difficult when there is no plan at all.

I will add commentary throughout the text. This commentary will provide further thoughts and suggestions for leading of the service. If you read carefully, however, the Order of Worship itself will teach you much that you need to know. For your convenience, a full order, without commentary, will be included in the appendix as well as a shorter order for the person whom you are visiting. The latter contains only the rubrics that they will need. After we move through the full order, I will suggest possible ways that it can be shortened if it should become necessary to do so.

Now, let us turn to the order.

AN ORDER FOR USE IN EXTENDED TABLE SERVICES (SERVER'S COPY)

The following portions are reprinted from The United Methodist Book of Worship, *copyright ©1992 by The United Methodist Publishing House: Opening Prayer, Invitation, Confession and Pardon, and Prayer after Communion. Used by permission.*

This ministry of the extended table, and the Order of Worship presented here, is conducted under the rites and rubrics of the United Methodist Church. It is endorsed by the Administrative Board of (this congregation) and occurs under the supervision of (our pastoral staff).

Commentary

Copyright permission for one time use by a local congregation is noted on the imprint page of *The United Methodist Book of Worship*. Preparing more permanent servers' copies that you would keep from visit to visit would require explicit permission from The United Methodist Publishing House. It may be well worth pursuing. In either case, the Order of Worship that you carry with you must clearly display a notice of permission to reprint. It should display a notice of denominational and local church endorsement as well. The endorsement implies that the Communion servers are accountable to the church and the understanding of the sacraments that it expresses in its rubrics and customs. Such notice also indicates that servers are receiving ongoing supervision (and support) within the local congregation. At the appropriate places, you would include the name of your congregation and the person(s) on the pastoral staff who supervise the ministry.

INTRODUCTORY RUBRICS

1. First dismissal scenario from the congregation's Service of Word and Table: The Communion sets will be given to you, perhaps by a deacon or Communion steward, after the congregation has received Communion and before the prayer after Communion. You will be dismissed to your visit and will depart while the congregation sings its final hymn.

2. Second dismissal scenario: Retrieve the elements after the congregational service and proceed to the visit as soon as possible.

3. Under either dismissal scenario, the Communion sets will be prepared for you, and they should include an adequate supply of the consecrated elements. If you think that you will need more than the usual amount, please notify the stewards ahead of time. Should you find yourself with an inadequate supply of consecrated elements, please notify the pastor. Under no circumstances should you serve unconsecrated elements, nor should you consecrate them yourself.

4. When you arrive at the visit site, greet your host as you enter his or her home or room. Find a table or flat surface (perhaps a coffee table, an end table, or even a TV tray) on which you can arrange the elements for the service. Set up for the service, putting the bread on the plate and small amounts of wine (or juice) in the cups.

5. You may converse some before the service begins, but you should try to keep such conversation to a minimum. Seek to begin the service as soon as possible after you arrive.

Commentary

As I have noted at various points, the home service is an extension of the congregational Service of Word and Table. It is as if we were moving the back row of the congregation into the community. Such understanding, however, needs a ritual form if it is to take root in the servers and the congregation. Of first importance is the commitment to use only Communion elements consecrated within the congregational worship service. In the United Methodist Church, we have decided that our pastors lead the Great Thanksgiving, which includes this petition spoken over the elements: "make them be for us the body and blood of Christ."[4] That petition is known as the epiclesis. As our scholars and leaders were developing our current form for the Great Thanksgiving, at first they considered a less explicit version of this epiclesis. Specifically this form appeared in the first version, published in 1972:

"Send the power of Your Holy Spirit on us,
   gathered here out of love for you,
   and on these gifts.

Help us know
   in the breaking of the bread
   and the drinking of this wine
   the presence of Christ
   who gave his body and blood for mankind."[5]

The church decided, however, that the 1972 form was not a strong enough affirmation of God's work. We believed that God wanted to do more than "help us know" something, so we moved to the current, bolder petition—"make them be for us the body and blood of Christ."[6] We believe God causes a change in the elements and that the change occurs in and through the Great Thanksgiving that the pastor proclaims in the midst of the gathered congregation with the congregation adding its "Amen." Thus, unconsecrated elements are inadequate, as are elements privately consecrated by a pastor in his or her office. All elements that will be used in the extended table visits should be on the altar-table during the Great Thanksgiving. If not all of them will fit there, then you may place some of them on a supplemental table directly in front of the altar-table.

Ideally, a deacon or steward will pack the home Communion sets while the rest of the congregation is being served. (Such sets can be purchased at various levels of quality, or members of the congregation can make quite handsome and useful sets. For a description of several possibilities, see the appendix.) Portions of bread can be torn from a loaf and placed in a container for transport and wine (juice) can be poured into vials or small cruets that can be sealed and safely transported. A pouring chalice—that is, a chalice equipped with a small spout for pouring—facilitates this work. If this preparation work is done at the altar in full view of the congregation, the assembly receives another visual reminder of the connection between Lord's Table and mission. Elements can also be taken to the sacristy after the Great Thanksgiving and the sets packed there. Sets could also be packed ahead of time and placed on the altar for the Great Thanksgiving.

The dismissal of the servers from the congregation is another important ritual moment. All benedictions proclaim the congregation's missional intention. We do not simply say, "Go in peace," but rather, "Go in peace, to love and serve the Lord." By giving a specific dismissal to the home Communion servers, the whole congregation claims their work as its own. "Sent Forth by God's Blessing" (UMH 664) makes a particularly apt musical accompaniment to their dismissal, especially this phrase from stanza one: "The service is ended, O now be extended, the fruits of our worship to all who believe."[7] If no formal dismissal is offered within the congregational service (see second dismissal scenario, above), at the least the prayers of the people (or pastoral prayer) should occasionally mention the servers as well as those who receive their ministry. Such prayers should become a regular practice in all congregations that develop an extended table ministry.

Should the names of those who will be visited be read within the congregation's service? Laurence Stookey has argued that these persons should be named as a way of affirming the unity of the church,[8] and I am persuaded by his argument. Nevertheless, since he published his book in 1993, we have become increasingly hesitant to name parishioners in public, especially elderly ones. Naming them publicly has a clear theological and spiritual benefit, but it might also draw attention to their vulnerable condition. While cognizant of the risks, I lean toward the benefit of reading their names. Otherwise they are easily forgotten and the Body of Christ diminished. Individual congregations and clergy, however, need to weigh this issue and decide what to do.

Introductory rubrics four and five are manifestly practical. Remember that most of the people whom you will visit are elderly, and they may be ill. Their energy level may not be very high, and after a hard week of work, your energy may be lagging a bit as well. So you want to prepare for the service and begin reasonably soon after you arrive. Do not be abrupt in your manner; rather be purposeful. Use the first fruits of your energy for the worship of God, and then you may converse further after the service is completed.

SERVICE OF THE WORD

Greeting
Give the following signal that the service is beginning.
Grace to you, and peace, in Jesus Christ our Lord. Amen.
This morning in our worship service, we celebrated the service of the Lord's Supper. We've come to bring you Communion from the same altar.

Opening Prayer
Invite those present to join in the prayer, and at least in the "Amen."
Almighty God, to you all hearts are open, all desires known, and from you no secrets are hidden. Cleanse the thoughts of our hearts by the inspiration of your Holy Spirit, that we may perfectly love you, and worthily magnify your holy name, through Christ our Lord. Amen.[9]

Commentary

The greeting fulfills a function similar to what the dismissal did within the congregational service. It expresses the connection between the extended service and the primary service.

Since liturgy is the work of the whole body of Christ, in all of our worship we invite people to participate actively, to sing the hymns and songs, to speak the responses, to join the unison prayers, to chant the Psalms, and to receive Holy Communion. Repeating key prayers and responses over time facilitates response at an even deeper level. For this reason, the extended table service uses the classic Anglican collect for purity, which has been a part of Methodist ritual texts since John Wesley and the beginning of the movement. Invite your communicant to pray it with you. Speak the prayer at an unhurried pace. Most persons will join right in. More than a few servers have been surprised to hear relatively unresponsive people begin reciting the phrases of such familiar prayers. Such is the formative power of classical prayer texts and a good reason for learning an ordinary while young.

Throughout your leadership, remember that the most basic liturgical response is the "Amen." Loosely translated, it means "Yes, you have spoken that prayer on my behalf and I agree." Thus, if your communicant can make no other response, at the least encourage him or her to say the "Amen."

Act of Praise
Sing or recite a verse (or verses) of a hymn or Psalm.

Scripture
Read one of the scriptures from the morning (Epistle or Gospel), introducing the reading with the following statement:
This morning we read from _____.
The leader or others present may offer comments on the lesson.

Prayer of Intercession
Offer a brief prayer for the person whom you are visiting. Also offer any concerns he/she may wish to raise. Encourage him/her to speak prayers as well.

Commentary

The Act of Praise is the first proper that you must provide. What will you do? I hope you will consider singing, perhaps a stanza or two from a hymn that you know reasonably well. Churches are one of the last remaining places where people sing aloud in public, ballparks being another.[10] Seriously, some of our deepest faith connections relate to the hymns that we have sung. Thus, I encourage you to push yourself beyond your reticence and offer the gift of hymn singing. More than one seemingly unresponsive person has stirred when someone sang "Amazing Grace" or "Joy to the World." If you will not sing, then (as the rubric says) at least speak the words of a hymn or song. But, I urge you to swallow your pride and sing.

As to scripture, read one of the lessons for the day; the one on which the sermon was based makes the best connection to the congregational service. While it is not necessary that you repeat the pastor's sermon for the day, you should have some conversation about the scripture for the day. What do you hear in it? It is good to ask the person whom you are visiting what she or he hears in the text as well; and yes, it is acceptable to quote your pastor.

At the intercessions, resist the temptation to pray merely for the needs of the person whom you are visiting. Invite communicants to name their concerns and to offer their prayers as well. Certainly persons need your prayers, but you may benefit from theirs also. Indeed, at the church where I trained my first group of home Communion servers, when they were ready to conduct their first visit, we called upon the woman who organized our church prayer phone tree. She had perhaps the most important prayer ministry in the church. Even if that is not the case in your situation, your host can participate fully in the prayers, again, at least to say the "Amen."

SERVICE OF COMMUNION

Invitation
The leader says the following:
Christ our Lord invites to his table all who love him and seek to grow into his likeness. Let us draw near with faith, make our humble confession, and prepare to receive this Holy Sacrament.[11]

Confession and Pardon
Invite those present to join in the entire prayer, and at least in the "Amen."
We do not presume to come to this your table, merciful Lord, trusting in our own goodness, but in your unfailing mercies. We are not worthy that you should receive us, but give your word and we shall be healed, through Jesus Christ our Lord. Amen.[12]

The leader continues as follows:
Hear the good news: Christ died for us while we were yet sinners; that is proof of God's love toward us. In the name of Jesus Christ, you are forgiven![13]

The Peace
Signs and words of God's peace are exchanged.[14]
The peace of the Lord be with you.

Commentary

"This Holy Mystery" calls for "the words of invitation" to be used, along with the confession and pardon sequence, each time the Lord's Supper is celebrated; otherwise, people may not properly understand the nature of Christ's call to the table.[15] Extended table Communion visits should follow this same rule. There is no need for Christians to wallow in their sin, but they must not take it lightly, either. Rather, sin is brought to light in confession, and pardon and grace to overcome its effects are given in the sacrament. Regardless of our age or condition, we never outgrow our need for this gospel. Thus the "Word and Table V" text proclaims it clearly, albeit with a slight difference from the invitation used in Word and Table services I and II. Each contains a call to confession. In each case, the passing of the peace follows confession. In those services I and II, the first sentence of the invitation contains the phrase, "who earnestly repent of their sin." That phrase is omitted in service V, but a call to confession is given nonetheless.[16]

Again, you should ask the communicant to speak the confession with you, but if that is not possible, invite him or her to participate in the prayer by speaking the "Amen." As a reminder, I have inserted a rubric to that effect. It is also possible that the person will want to make more extensive and personal confession, and there is ample precedent for sick and dying people doing so. You should neither encourage nor discourage such confessions; in the rare case that a particularly serious sin were to be confessed to you, you may wish to refer the case to your pastor. According to Methodist ritual and theology, however, a layperson may proclaim the statement of pardon, and you should do so if confession has been made. That pardon is no more, yet no less, than a proclamation of the gospel, and we all need to hear it.

In like manner, the passing of the peace is an essential part of the Communion ritual and may be an especially important means of grace for people who are isolated or living with illnesses. We tend to recoil from the sick and ignore the elderly, but our ritual calls us to touch them. You should do so discreetly and carefully, yet warmly, looking directly into the other's eyes as you say, "The peace of the Lord be with you." All present should share such greetings with each other, and if it takes a few minutes to do so, then it is time well spent.[17] What's your hurry?

The Lord's Prayer
The leader says the following, joined by the others present:
Before we receive Communion, let us pray together as Jesus taught us saying, **"Our Father . . ."**

Giving the Bread and Cup
Serve all present who wish to receive. At the least, the home Communion servers should receive with the homebound member.
What if you have a shortage of Communion cups, or of wine (juice)? For example, say that you have five small cups but seven people who wish to receive. In that case, some may receive by intinction. The principal recipient of the visit, however, should be served first and should have a cup of his or her own.
Administer the elements with the following or similar words:
The body of Christ, given for you. **Amen.**
The blood of Christ, given for you. **Amen.**[18]

Commentary

The Great Thanksgiving would come at this point in the congregational service. It is omitted in an extended table service. Again, United Methodist polity
reserves the leadership of this prayer to the pastor. The extended service
does, however, retain the Lord's Prayer, which repeats our intention to participate in forgiveness and reconciliation along with our desire to receive the
nourishment that God gives.

As we finish the prayer, we proceed to Communion. Who should
receive? Answers to that question vary by denomination and circumstance,
and such is also the case in extended table Communion. In the United
Methodist Church, we insist that "All who respond in faith to the invitation
are to be welcomed,"[19] but what does it mean to give an invitation in an
extended table setting, especially in a public setting like a hospital or nursing home? What does response to the invitation look like in such settings?

Let us begin with the simplest case, that of a service occurring in the living room of a homebound church member. The invitation from your parishioner makes that room something like an extension of the church's sanctuary
and Communion rail. It is altogether possible that when you arrive at their
home you will find other visitors present, especially if you visit on the Lord's
Day. What should you do? You may offer to return at a more opportune time,
but if they insist that you remain, then it is altogether proper to ask those
present to participate in the service. As we do in church, let the Communion
invitation interpret itself; if persons ask questions about it, then explain our
rubrics to the best of your ability. You may have to divide the elements carefully. Even a relatively modest piece of bread, say two cubic inches, can be
divided with care among as many as six or seven persons. With similar care,
wine (juice) in a small flask or cruet can be apportioned across six or seven
small individual Communion cups. Indeed, a few drops can make for a valid
Communion, and one should avoid overfilled cups anyway. As the rubrics
suggest, if there is a shortage of juice, I suggest serving an individual cup to
the primary person (or persons) whom you came to visit and then serving
the others by intinction. Normally, you will commune with the person you
are visiting, for no one should commune alone. You could, however, abstain
if supplies appear low.

Hospitals and nursing homes present an institutional scenario different
from the living room. There you find yourself performing sacramental ministry
in a semiprivate setting, and so you should focus on the person whom you
have come to visit, including others only if they address you and specifically

ask for your ministry. Use common sense when you serve people in hospitals. Do not hesitate to ask a nurse for help, first identifying yourself and then your purpose in being there. If you find the person whom you came to serve lying down, then ask that she or he be raised to a sitting position. If you are not sure if it is physically safe for a person to receive Communion, then ask the nurse. Given our religiously pluralistic society, it may be necessary carefully to explain to hospital personnel what "receive Communion" means, as in "I will feed her a morsel of bread and a small sip of wine (juice)." Pay careful heed to NPO (from the Latin *nil per os* or "nothing by mouth") orders. When a person is not allowed to swallow, normally a sign will have been posted to that effect.

Perhaps ironically, the doctrine of concomitance, that is, the belief that full Communion in Christ is received in either the consecrated bread or wine, can be helpful in some situations. Protestants are accustomed to receiving Communion "in both kinds," that is, in both the bread and wine and have been since the reforms of the sixteenth century. It is an important commitment, one that we believe fulfills Christ's commandment to eat and drink in remembrance of him (1 Corinthians 11: 23-26; Matthew 26: 26-29). It may be necessary, however, to relax this commitment when dealing with the Communion of the infirm. This concomitance doctrine, admittedly developed to justify withholding of the cup from the laity, can mean that a small sip of wine, or even a drop applied to the lips, is full Communion in Christ. Some, however, cannot even receive at that level. In that case, something akin to ocular Communion—that is, Communion received through gazing at the consecrated host—could be done, perhaps with the host lightly touched to the person's lips while you say, "The Body of Christ, given for you." Above all, use good common sense, and when in doubt, ask questions. In most cases, of course, everyone present will receive Communion in both kinds, in the bread and the wine (juice).

Commentary

The prayer after Communion briefly addresses some of the themes normally covered in a Great Thanksgiving: the life, death, and resurrection of Jesus Christ and thanksgiving for the gift of the holy meal. That this prayer occurs after Communion, however, demonstrates that it has no consecratory intent, and thus a layperson may properly offer it.

The service concludes with a short blessing. It can be easily memorized and thus should be delivered while looking at the person addressed. Remaining matters are addressed in "rubrics following the service." After the

Prayer After Communion
The leader prays as follows:
Most bountiful God, we give you thanks for the world you have created, for the gift of life, and for giving yourself to us in Jesus Christ,
whose holy life, suffering and death, and glorious resurrection have
delivered us from slavery to sin and death. We thank you that in the
power of your Holy Spirit you have fed us in this Sacrament, united us
with Christ, and given us a foretaste of your heavenly banquet. We are
your children, and yours is the glory, now and for ever; through Jesus
Christ our Lord. **Amen.**[20]

Blessing
The leader addresses those gathered with the following words:
The grace of the Lord Jesus Christ, and the love of God, and the com-
munion of the Holy Spirit be with you. **Amen.**[21]

RUBRICS FOLLOWING THE SERVICE

1. If it seems appropriate, spend a few moments in conversation.

2. When your visits for the day are completed, consume any
    unused elements. A small amount of wine (juice) and crumbs
    may be returned to the earth, perhaps in your flowerbed.
    Consecrated Communion elements should not be thrown in
    the trash.

3. Please report completed visits on the form provided.

service is the time for further conversation; again, be prudent as well as hon-
est about your own schedule. When I make calls, even to persons in hospital rooms, I notice that many subtly take on the role of host, and that role
take energy that some persons may not have to spend. Be sensitive to your
context. In most cases, you will want to stay for a short time and then be on
your way; ten minutes is probably more than enough.

Care for remaining Communion elements with respect. Although United
Methodists have not focused on a literal change in the elements and have at
times stridently disavowed it, we do not regard consecrated elements as
empty signs. Throwing them in the trash is impious. We should handle them
with at least as much care as our dinner leftovers. Prevailing ecumenical

wisdom says that it is best to consume what remains, and indeed it is the practice least likely to wound the conscience of others.

The third rubric speaks to accountability and working under supervision. Thus, a record of the visit should be filed, including any information that the pastor should know. The appendix includes a sample report form.

ADDITIONAL RUBRICS

1. Always remember that you are a guest in someone else's home. If someone hesitates to receive this ministry from you, remind him or her that your ministry is endorsed by your congregation and supervised by your pastor. If they still refuse to receive you, do not argue with them. Please let your pastor know about any such refusals.

2. Since we do not recognize a reserved sacrament in the United Methodist Church, you should plan to make your visits on the day of the congregational service, or on the next day at the very least.

3. Home visits should be scheduled ahead of time. It is a good idea to call ahead when planning to visit in nursing homes. It is possible that other activities may be scheduled at the time you hope to visit.

4. Observe hospital visiting hours.

5. Serve only the consecrated elements given to you at the congregational service. Using unconsecrated elements, or laypersons attempting to consecrate more, violates the trust on which this ministry is based.

6. Preserve confidentiality. You may, however, share information with your pastor. If you see evidence of abuse or neglect, inform your pastor immediately.

7. Above all, remember that you represent Christ and this church. Go prayerfully, in Christ's joy and peace.

Commentary

I call this additional set of rubrics the "Ecclesiastical Do's and Don'ts for Home Communion Servers." They represent common-sense church etiquette; but given the fine line that exists between civilization and chaos, reminders can be helpful.

Rubric 1

As I have noted earlier, using laypersons to carry Communion to persons outside the congregational service is a relatively new practice for United Methodists. We can expect that some people will accept the new practice better than others. When congregations begin practicing extended table, those who will receive the ministry (primarily those on the congregation's homebound list) should be offered a clear explanation of the practice and its rationale, including its many benefits. As a pastor, I found it helpful to assure these people that I would continue visiting them on a regular basis as I vowed to do at the time of my ordination.[22] Those people who decline extended table ministry should not be assigned to the visitors; thus the problem of someone rejecting your visit is not likely to arise. Persons should, however, always be afforded freedom to decline Communion.[23]

Rubrics 2, 3, and 4

As I also note in other places, it is not easy to maintain the distinction between reserved sacrament, which United Methodists do not permit, and extended table, which we now endorse. Clarity about our intentions is essential, but ritual practices that appear to contradict our stated intentions will erode the distinction. Waiting several days between consecration and the visit will make it difficult to defend a distinction; thus I offer the rubric about making the visit soon after the congregational service, the next day at the latest. Anything beyond that time frame should be handled in a latter week, or through a Communion visit by the pastor, which would, of course, involve praying the Great Thanksgiving.

As noted, home visits should be scheduled. I suggest assigning that duty to a church secretary or staff person, or to a volunteer who works with the visitation team. Asking the pastor to do such basic secretarial work is not good stewardship of his or her gifts and calling.

Rubric 5

This rubric re-emphasizes the point made earlier, that one should use only consecrated elements (see introductory rubric #3).

Rubric 6

The discussion about confidentiality and referrals is rooted in the Golden Rule as well as basic common sense. What do we want other people to do with the information that they learn about us? When you enter people's homes and minister to them, you will inevitably learn things about them— both by inference and by direct communication. As a matter of basic Christian compassion and love, you should not share what you learn. It should emerge neither in conversation nor in public prayers, such as, "Lord, you know Mrs. Smith has an appointment on Wednesday morning to have her bunions removed, and she's anxious . . ." Congregational intercessions are important, but perhaps a quiet whispering of the name will suffice; God knows the details. As noted, you may discreetly pass information on to your pastor, who stands within the circle of confidentiality. You must inform your pastor if you see evidence of abuse or neglect. I do not mean to alarm you or burden you by raising this issue, nor do I want you to go looking for trouble. The vast majority of your visits will be pleasant and routine, but if you see something that looks like trouble, inform your pastor and then let the matter rest in his or her hands. If you do so, you have done your duty and completed your task.

Rubric 7

I have included this one to remind us about the reason for all rubrics. They try to express the wisdom we have gained about Christian practices. Rubrics are necessary, but their goal is always joy and peace in Jesus Christ, nothing less.

ADDENDUM: GUIDELINES ON ABBREVIATING THE SERVICE

The service that I describe above is quite flexible, and participants can easily complete it in twenty to twenty five-minutes, even if they do everything appointed. I commend the full service to you. One should not shorten it merely for the sake of convenience. It may be necessary, however, to abbreviate it, particularly in the case of persons living with Alzheimer's disease and other forms of dementia. In doing so, try to maintain the classic relationship of Word and Table, while trusting the power of familiar texts. The following represents one possible shorter version:

- Scripture reading (possibly as short as one or two verses);
- Prayer of Confession, with Pardon;

- Lord's Prayer;
- Communion;
- Extemporaneous Prayer, following Communion.

In this order, Word and Table is offered along with confession. You might use scripture texts that may have been memorized, such as John 3: 16-17 or Psalm 23. The familiar cadences of the Lord's Prayer may evoke some recognition, as may the giving of the elements accompanied by the traditional words. As noted before, invite the person whom you are visiting to join the prayers, and at least in the "Amen."

The following represents the briefest possible abbreviated form:

- Scripture verse;
- Lord's Prayer;
- Communion.

In this case, we understand that the Lord's Prayer contains a prayer for pardon: "Forgive us our trespasses . . . etc."

You may now prepare to begin a ministry of home Communion serving. Do not be afraid of making mistakes; doubtless you will make some, but you will be a blessing as well. That is far more important than spending time worrying about possible mistakes. In chapter five, we will discuss issues to consider in beginning an extended table ministry within your congregation. But first, I want you to hear some testimonies from persons who have been involved in this ministry.

Questions and Topics for Discussion

1. Read through the order of service, paying careful attention to the rubrics. Visualize leading the various parts of the service. Do any of the rubrics confuse you? Raise questions about anything in them that you don't understand or that you can't imagine yourself doing.

2. Hold a practice and reflection session for your class. Set aside approximately three hours for the process, which will unfold as follows:

   - Organize visitation groups of two or three to be sent on Communion calls. (These calls will be made on real church members, preferably persons on the church homebound list.

Appointments will be made ahead of time and driving directions provided to each place. Those visited should represent relatively uncomplicated cases.)

- The visitation groups will meet and assign leadership to the various parts of the service. Make choices as necessary. (Take approximately thirty minutes for these first two steps.)
- Hold a short Service of Word and Table, led by an ordained minister. (Thirty minutes.)
- At the close of the service, send the groups for their visits, appointing a time for their return. (Depending on local geography and traffic patterns, I suggest reconvening seventy-five minutes after they leave.)
- **Pastors should refrain from accompanying the visitation teams. They'll learn more if they go on their own.**
- Return for reflection on the process, including any troubleshooting that may be necessary. (Forty-five minutes.)

3. As they prepare for the Communion call, visitation groups should ask themselves the following questions:

- Who will lead the service of the Word?
   What will be done for the Act of Praise?
   What scripture will be read?
- Who will lead the Communion service?
- What remaining questions do we have, and how shall we resolve them?

4. After the groups return from their visit, the reflection session should unfold as follows:

- Ask people to describe their experience of leading a Communion call. Gather general questions and comments.
- Ask them to describe what went well.
- Ask them to describe any problems or challenges that they encountered. Discuss possible solutions to problems or make a commitment to look for solutions. Did anyone see anything he or she should report to the pastor?
- As appropriate, offer prayers of thanksgiving for the experience you have just had. Offer intercessions for those who were visited and for those who visited them.

Notes

1. Sometimes, texts that function like rubrics are spoken aloud, as when the priest reading from *The Book of Common Prayer* says the following:

Ye who do truly and earnestly repent you of your sins, and are in love and charity with your neighbors, and intend to live a new life, following the commandments of God, and walking from henceforth in his holy ways: Draw near with faith and make your humble confession to almighty God, devoutly kneeling. (See *The Book of Common Prayer*. [New York: Church Hymnal Corporation, 1979], 331.)

Today, when congregations hear the words "Draw near with faith," they hear it as an invitation to take on a change of heart through repentance. However, when this text first became a part of the English liturgy, in the sixteenth century, the intent was more literal. When they heard it, those who intended to participate in Communion were expected to "draw near." They would rise, enter the chancel, and gather around the altar. In today's liturgies, the call to exchange signs of peace and reconciliation functions as a spoken rubric. It calls us to move, and not just to sit there and say, "Yes, reconciliation is a good idea."

2. *The United Methodist Hymnal* (Nashville, Tennessee: The United Methodist Publishing House, 1989), 6. This prayer is classically known as "The Collect for Purity." From "A Service of Word and Table I" © 1972, 1980, 1985, 1989, The United Methodist Publishing House. Used by permission.

3. *The United Methodist Book of Worship* (Nashville, Tennessee: The United Methodist Publishing House, 1992), 51-53.

4. *The United Methodist Hymnal*, 1989, 10.

5. *The Sacrament of the Lord's Supper, An Alternate Text (Music Edition)* (Nashville: The United Methodist Publishing House, 1972, 1975), 16-17. From "Sacrament of the Lord's Supper (Alternate Text) Music Edition" ©1972, 1975 The United Methodist Publishing House. Used by permission.

6. *The United Methodist Hymnal*, 1989, 10. Used by permission.

For a full account of this movement in the epiclesis and the discussion surrounding it, see Robert Brian Peiffer, *How Contemporary Liturgies Evolve: The Revision of United Methodist Liturgical Texts (1968-1988)* (Unpublished Ph. D. dissertation, University of Notre Dame, 1993), 30.

7. Omer Westendorf, "Sent Forth by God's Blessing," text ©1964, World Library Publications, Franklin Park, Illinois. www.wlpmusic.com (800) 566-6150. Used by permission.

The text may be found in *The United Methodist Hymnal*, 664.

My student Debra McKnight pointed me to this stanza and its potential use as a dismissal for home Communion servers.

8. Laurence Hull Stookey, *Eucharist, Christ's Feast in the Church* (Nashville: Abingdon Press, 1993), 156-57.

9. *The United Methodist Hymnal*, 1989, 6. Used by permission.

10. Of late, even "The Star-Spangled Banner" is usually sung as a solo piece, and, I might add, not always particularly well. But I digress. Thanks to the late

Harry Caray and the influence of Wrigley Field, however, at the seventh inning stretch in many ballparks, the "congregation" sings "Take Me Out to the Ballgame."

11. *The United Methodist Book of Worship*, 1992, 51. Used by permission.

12. Ibid. Used by permission.

13. Ibid., 52. From "A Service of Word and Table V with Persons Who Are Sick or Homebound" ©1976, 1980 by Abingdon; ©1985, 1987, 1992 The United Methodist Publishing House. Used by permission.

14. Ibid. Used by permission.

15. "This Holy Mystery, A United Methodist Understanding of Holy Communion," *The Book of Resolutions of the United Methodist Church*, 2004, page 899. Copyright © 2004, The United Methodist Publishing House. Used by permission.

16. *The United Methodist Book of Worship*, 1992, 35, 40, 51.

17. See a discussion of such a passing of the peace in my book *Sacraments and Discipleship, Understanding Baptism and the Lord's Supper in a United Methodist Context* (Nashville, Tennessee: Discipleship Resources, 2001), 114. See also pages 82-84.

18. *The United Methodist Book of Worship*, 1992, 53.

19. "This Holy Mystery," 900. Used by permission.

20. *The United Methodist Book of Worship*, 1992, 53. Used by permission.

21. Ibid., 53. Used by permission.

22. The historic questions addressed to candidates for ordination as elder ask, "Will you visit from house to house?" From *The Book of Discipline of the United Methodist Church-2004*, ¶ 336.15. Copyright © 2004 by the United Methodist Publishing House. Used by permission.

23. "Response to the invitation is always voluntary, and care needs to be taken to ensure that no one feels pressured to participate or conspicuous for not doing so."

"This Holy Mystery," 903. Used by permission.

Interlude: Testimonies from Home Communion Servers

As Christians, we believe that God is actively at work in the world and that we participate in that work. One can argue, I suppose, that God can work in other ways, and we might concede the point; but the God we read about in scripture and church history works through people. When God wanted to liberate the children of Israel from slavery, God called Moses. When God decided to send the Son into the world, God called Mary, who agreed to be part of the story. She said, "Here I am, the servant of the Lord; let it be with me according to your word" (Luke 1:38). In the biblical narrative, God works through people. In like manner, when God wants to reconnect homebound church members to the Body of Christ, God calls people like you, inviting you to participate in this work of healing and redemption. Doing so is a great privilege, but it is not for the faint of heart. Working with God, one will encounter real suffering and pain, not to mention occasional boredom and homes where the thermostat is set higher than we prefer. Yes, we carry the cross in ways large and small, but in the midst of sacrifice we also experience the joy of new creation and resurrection. Wonderful and surprising things happen where God is at work, and you are privileged to see them. Such is the adventure of answering God's call.

But you have heard enough from me for a while. Now I want you to listen to a few stories from the ministry of some other home Communion servers.

From Paula T. Simpson, Epworth United Methodist Church, Rehoboth Beach, Delaware

I have been serving Communion to those at home or in retirement homes for about nine years. I have had many memorable experiences, some deeply moving and some on the funny side. Something that I have learned is that whatever happens, particularly when you are serving the elderly, is okay. What matters is that you are there to bring them a sense of relationship with God and God's caring. We don't have to say the words perfectly or follow the ritual exactly. The whole thing needs to come from your heart with God's blessing.

On one occasion, after a lovely, quiet, and spirit-filled time together, after the meal had been served, a lovely thing happened. At this time, unbeknownst to the family, I was feeling rather low myself due to a serious illness in my own family. The wife began to sing in a sweet, soft voice, "Fill My Cup, Lord." She sang it all the way through, never missing a word. Not only did I feel like I had ministered to this couple, but she was able to minister to me in a very meaningful way. The song was just what I needed to hear at the time.

On another occasion when I was with the same couple, ages ninety-four and eighty-six, the husband put a little mechanical bird on the table where I had set Communion. He wound it up, and that bird chirruped and walked all around the table during our little worship time. Nothing they could do would stop it. Afterwards, I came to the realization that "it was what it was." I was there, the couple felt cared for, and God's Spirit was with us too—maybe in the form of a blue bird.

It has also become our practice to take Communion monthly to a local assisted-living facility. Another person usually accompanies me. When we first began to take Communion to this community, we drew just three to five folks and that was fine. Then one of the ladies who attended regularly began to invite others. Last month we had fourteen. We sat and visited with them afterwards and heard such things as where they were from and what church they had attended, how long it had been since they had been served Communion, how it made them remember what it was like to go to church and the good feelings that came with that, and especially simply "Thank you for coming," over and over again. There is no personal reward greater than the feeling that God has given us the privilege of serving in God's name.[1]

From Lisa A. Griffith, O.S.L., Emmanuel United Methodist Church, White Sulphur Springs, West Virginia

One Sunday after worship, I was to deliver Communion to the White Sulphur Springs Family Care Center. We had four parishioners in the care center. I was extremely tired and wanted to go home and rest. My mother said she would go with me, if I wanted. All I kept thinking was that if I were in the Family Care Center, [I would want] someone to visit and bring me Communion.

So, Mother and I went to the first person on our list, who was not in the room. The second person on the list was asleep, but the third person was awake. This is a lady who always greeted you with a wonderful smile despite the pain she was in because of her cancer. She so looked forward to receiving Communion and visiting with us.

I was glad I had taken the time to do this for her. Not only was it very meaningful to her, but also it made me realize I would have missed a wonderful opportunity to do my ministry. The lady passed away a short time after this, and I was happy that I was able to share the Lord's Table with her before she died.

In our busy lives, we sometimes forget those who would love to be in worship with us and receive Communion. Yes, [visiting them] can be an inconvenience if one has many things planned for one's day. But one misses more if we do not remember who we are and what we are supposed to be doing.

We have a parishioner who is homebound because she is on oxygen twenty-four hours a day and is too weak to walk very far. This is a woman who gave over thirty years to the same establishment as my mother where they both went full steam (twelve to fourteen-hour days). Now the lady sits in a chair in her living room waiting for loved ones to call or come by for a visit. When Mother and I take her Communion, you would think we had brought her a bag of gold. She forgets her infirmities for a little while, and Mother and she talk about different topics they have in common. She is always very appreciative that we give up our time to visit and take her Communion.[2]

From April Galbraith, Trinity United Methodist Church, Roaring Spring, Pennsylvania

We shared Holy Communion with Rosie. She shared Christ with us. She shared her faith journey, including the days, when alone and sick, she felt the very presence of Christ in the room. We came away feeling strengthened and renewed.

Our ministry with Rosie is only one of the many uplifting faith experiences the home Communion servers have witnessed in the past year. About one year ago, Trinity United Methodist Church began to develop a more holistic way of extending our Communion table to members of our congregation. Laypersons, in teams of two, take the consecrated Communion elements to shut-in members following the Sunday morning worship service. The names of the servers and the people they visit are announced as a part of the worship service so that the congregation can include them in their prayers.

Although the teams serve shut-in members, the servers gain even more. As the teams spend time with homebound members and their families, everyone involved shares life experiences and develops friendships. Again, the servers usually feel that they receive far more than they give.

Even in difficult situations, the rewards are still present. On a recent visit to an Alzheimer patient, we wondered if this individual would understand or even participate in the sharing of the Communion elements. The patient was wandering the halls of the nursing home, but we were eventually able to gather this individual, [his] spouse, and a friend.

As we said the prayer and gave the bread and juice, the individual's blank eyes began to focus on the elements. This person, who moments before had seemed totally unaware of the surroundings, seemed to participate actively in the Sacrament. As he received the body and blood of Christ, without prompting, the patient's eyes began to twinkle.[3]

From Sybil B. Wolff and Richard C. Wolff, M.D., St. Andrew's United Methodist Church, San Antonio, Texas

When we lost our part-time minister from retirement and I realized that our members in nursing homes or at home were unable to come to church, I asked Pastor George if we could take Communion to them. He then set up a procedure and held a class teaching us what to do and what to say.

My wife and I found the experience very rewarding and revealing. We found that several of our members were not having any visitors, except us. They did not want us to leave after we served Communion. In Alzheimer's units, we offered Communion to anyone in the area where our church member happened to be. We served as many as eight people in addition to our member. After several months, we found that one of these patients was the wife of a deceased Methodist minister. She was always so grateful when we served her.

We have been taking Communion to a former member of our church choir. Her husband does nothing else but spend all afternoons with her and has no other human contact except with his granddaughter. He is so grateful for the human contact and news from his church.

This type of service, as is mission work, is more rewarding to we who serve than to those whom we serve.[4]

From Paul Lewis, Trinity United Methodist Church, Eugene, Oregon

We started taking out home Communion a couple of years ago and have found it very rewarding to both the taker and the receiver. I always try to take along the bulletin from the day's church service, along with the current *Upper Room* and any other pertinent information I may have. Before serving I just visit a bit, bringing them bits of news about the church and about members whom they may know: illnesses, weddings, funerals, vacations, special services, etc. After serving, I stay and chat for a little while.

After returning from the visit, I leave a note for Pastor Pamela about the visit and relay any requests from the member, if any. I especially try to relay any need they may have, or whether they appear to be depressed or could benefit from a visit from the pastor. To me this is one of the most rewarding things I do, and the other members of the team have said the same thing.[5]

You have now heard these stories from a sampling of lay home Communion servers. I hope they will inspire you to offer your own testimony. Taking Communion to church members who cannot attend worship is important for many clergy as well. As I have said at various points, there is ample room for both clergy and lay members to do this ministry. In that spirit, I share this story from Pastor John Dromazos of First United Methodist Church, Chambersburg, Pennsylvania. On the day before my father died, Pastor John shared Communion with him. It was *viaticum* in the classic sense, and I am grateful that he offered it.

From John J. Dromazos, pastor, First United Methodist Church, Chambersburg, Pennsylvania

In my ministry, I have had unique opportunities to celebrate Holy Communion. Some have been at weddings while others have been in someone's home. They all stand out in my memory. One that will forever stand out will be the one with John and Joanne Stamm on World Communion

Sunday, the day before John's death at Menno Haven Nursing facility. Joanne asked me if I would give John Communion. Timothy Baer, our district superintendent, was there also. I blessed the elements, and Tim and I gave the sacrament to John on a plastic spoon with bread and grape juice. Then the three of us received. I tell you, it was a holy moment as I knew that God was present, blessing his servant, John Stamm, who was to be received into his presence in a few short hours. That experience showed me the profound mystery ever present in the receiving of the bread and cup. May you discover the sense of mystery the next time you accept the invitation to receive this means of grace.[6]

Notes

1. Unpublished attachment to email sent to the author from Paula Simpson, June 14, 2007. The attachment is titled "Serving Home Communion to the Home Bound."

2. Email from Lisa A. Griffith, O.S.L., sent to the author, June 6, 2007.

3. Originally published as follows: April Galbraith, "Sharing Home Communion, Roaring Spring Church Discovers the Joy of Sharing," *The Link* (Altoona District Edition), July 1996, W3.

4. Email from Richard C. Wolff , M.D., sent to the author, July 13, 2007.

5. Email from Paul Lewis sent to the author, June 7, 2007.

6. John J. Dromazos, "Reflections from Pastor John," Newsletter, First United Methodist Church, Chambersburg, Pennsylvania (November 2007). Used by permission.

5

Getting Started in Your Congregation

The ministry of home Communion serving is rooted in the Baptismal Covenant, both through the vows that we make there and through the promises that God makes to us. Thus, it exists in a mutually supportive and accountable relationship with the rest of the church and its work. In this short chapter, I will propose a shape for such support and accountability. I will do so under the following three headings:

- Placing home Communion serving in the midst of congregational life;
- Recruiting, building, and maintaining a ministry group for home Communion servers;
- Administrative tasks related to home Communion serving.

Placing Home Communion Serving in the Midst of Congregational Life

Home Communion serving needs the support and encouragement of the pastor along with that of the entire congregation. Strong theological foundations are essential to developing such a relationship. As we have noted earlier, the church has been working to unlearn more than a millennium of clericalism, that is, to unlearn the habits that developed from the clergy making the major decisions and doing most of the ministry. Under those old assumptions, priests and pastors led all of the home Communion visits, and most laypersons assumed that such was the proper work of pastors. Liturgical scholars and others have now come to different, more biblically-rooted theological conclusions, but this newer, ancient-modern pattern will seem strange to some. It may even seem vaguely out of order. Furthermore, as people learn new roles they will make mistakes, sometimes unwittingly, sometimes not. What can be done? As to mistakes, I am reminded of the sage advice given by Catholic liturgical scholar Aidan Kavanagh. He insisted that worrying about making mistakes is one of the primary mistakes that a liturgical leader can make.[1] He was not encouraging sloppy leadership, of course, but he wanted to discourage a stifling preoccupation with one's own performance. As to trust between clergy and laity, we build it through fellowship and communication, with the pastor wholeheartedly supporting the ministry of the laity, and the laity giving a like support to their pastor.

When we firmly root our understanding of ministry in the Baptismal Covenant, we call each person to discern and exercise his or her ministry while respecting and supporting that of others (see 1 Corinthians 12). According to that spirit, each person within the home Communion ministry, clergy or lay, must know his or her role and then stay within it. As we noted earlier, pastors preside at the Lord's Table. They gather the community and give voice to the Great Thanksgiving, but then they must remember that the meal belongs not to them, but to the Lord and the whole church. It is the Lord's Supper and not the pastor's supper. Thus, pastors should delegate serving roles to deacons and laity and should receive their Communion at the hand of another. Delegation is not, however, abdication. While the pastor's role in home Communion serving moves away from the earlier pattern of clerical dominance, it is important that she or he remain engaged with this ministry. Appropriate pastoral teaching and supervision will help the lay servers become more knowledgeable and more attentive disciples. Moreover, the pastor remains the pastor of those people on the congregation's home-bound list and should continue to make occasional visits.

Public recognition and support of the home Communion servers by the pastors and others will help situate this ministry at the heart of congregational life and will affirm commitment to a newer, more holistic paradigm for ministry. What might such support look like? The public prayers offered by the pastor and the rest of the church occasionally should mention the work of the home Communion group. The congregation can also hold occasional commissioning rites for persons involved in this work, just as they might do for its Sunday school teachers and mission teams. The following rite includes portions adapted from "An Order for Commitment to Christian Service" printed in *The United Methodist Book of Worship*.[2] Worship leaders could use it on the first Sunday that the home Communion servers make visits, thus placing the blessing of the servers in direct relation to the exercise of their service. The order could be repeated occasionally, perhaps annually, as new Communion servers are trained and ready to begin their work.

AN ORDER FOR THE COMMISSIONING OF HOME COMMUNION SERVERS:

Let this service be observed after the congregation has received Holy Communion, and before the Prayer after Communion.
The pastor shall call the new Communion servers to the chancel rail.
After they arrive, the pastor says the following:
Jesus said, ". . . I was hungry and you gave me food, I was thirsty and you gave me something to drink . . ." (Matthew 25:35). Paul taught, "the body (of Christ) is one and has many members, and all the members of the body, though many, are one body" (1 Corinthians 12:12). Dear brothers and sisters, you have been called to fulfill the ministry of a home Communion server. Will you perform that ministry according to the rites, rubrics, and customs of the United Methodist Church?
The servers respond:

I/We will.
The pastor continues, using either form one or two.

1. If the names of those to be visited that day are not read publicly.

Today (*read the name of each server, continuing until all have been named*) will carry the sacrament to homebound persons who belong to this church. In doing so, (*he/she/they*) will extend the ministry of this table.

2. If the names of those to be visited are read publicly.

Today (*name of server or serving team*) will carry the sacrament to the home(s) of (*name[s] of homebound member[s]*).

Each is read in turn, naming all servers and their specific destinations. After all of the names have been read, the pastor says:

In doing so, *(he/she/they)* will extend the ministry of this table.

The pastor or deacon hands a Communion set to each server or serving team. When finished, the pastor says the following:

In the name of this congregation I commend you to this work and pledge to you our prayers, encouragement, and support. May the Holy Spirit guide and strengthen you, that in this and in all things you may do God's will in the service of Jesus Christ.[3]

Let us pray.

Almighty God, look with favor upon *(name or these persons)* who reaffirm(s) commitment to follow Christ and follow in his name. Give *(him, her, each of them)* courage, patience, and vision; and strengthen us all in our Christian vocation of witness to the world and of service to others; through Jesus Christ our Lord. **Amen.**[4]

Prayer after Communion (e.g., see UMH, p. 11) and final hymn may follow, during which the servers exit the sanctuary and proceed to their visit(s).

Recruiting, Building, and Maintaining a Ministry Group for Home Communion Servers

How should the church recruit home Communion servers? One could make a general appeal, but such appeals tend to be rather ineffective; moreover, they are not very discerning. Some people will not make effective or trustworthy home Communion servers. As you read biblical call stories, note that in many of them people are addressed directly. God spoke to the young Jeremiah and said, "Before I formed you in the womb I knew you, and before you were born I consecrated you; I appointed you a prophet to the nations" (Jeremiah 1:5). The disciples followed Jesus after he specifically called *them* to fish for people (Mark 1: 16-20). In like manner, pastors and other leaders should pray for guidance and then go looking for people whom they believe will make good servers. Consider asking Lay Speakers and those who have completed DISCIPLE Bible Study courses. As you look for suitable people, ask questions like the following:

- Who is a good listener and is willing to take time with people?
- Who has a deep commitment to the Eucharist and its traditions?
- Whom are we overlooking?

When you have identified such people, visit them and share what you have observed about them. Tell them that you think they would do good work as home Communion servers.

Having found people to serve, there are two ways to form them for this task; the two ways are complementary and not mutually exclusive. The first involves offering classes that use resources like *Extending the Table*. One learns the history of this practice, along with its biblical and theological foundations. Then one receives specific instruction in doing it. This text provides this information. Other books and texts, like "This Holy Mystery" (and various resources referenced in the endnotes), will further deepen your understanding. Nevertheless, formation for ministry involves more than learning facts and theories, techniques and skills, essential as those may be. Effective trainers also take on the ethos of a practice, its mindset and perspective, its spirituality; they become ministers. Thus comes the second pathway to formation as a home Communion server: Mentor persons in this work. As you develop a cadre of servers, consider pairing new servers with more experienced ones. Become an evangelist for this practice. Since love for Christ and his ministry is contagious, perhaps caught more than taught, invite people to join you in this work. Then let the Spirit work. If you are going on a home Communion visit, invite someone from the church to accompany you, perhaps someone from your Sunday school class or someone in the church youth group or confirmation class. After obtaining proper supervisory clearance and parental permission, some fourth and fifth graders might profitably accompany teams on their visits. Again, forming people for ministry involves both formal instruction and apprenticeship, and formation can begin at a young age.

The initial period of formation is not the end of the process, either. Retaining persons in any type of ministry requires ongoing support and encouragement, a dynamic that the church has sometimes failed to practice. Remember that all Christian ministry is countercultural, that it runs against the consumerist values that prevail in our culture. That people can speak of the fulfillment they experience in giving themselves for others is evidence that the gospel has already formed them, at least to some extent. Nevertheless, servants of the gospel inevitably face discouragement and even disillusionment, which can begin for any number of reasons. Sometimes people do not respond in a gracious manner. Sometimes they do not respond at all. Nursing homes can be depressing places—too hot, too impersonal, too much like death waiting to happen. People need steady support if they are to continue ministering over time. Thus, home Communion servers should form a ministry group that meets occasionally for prayer and mutual encouragement, for continuing study and problem solving. The group should meet at least quarterly and perhaps as often as monthly. They might consider holding an occasional meal together, which might also include celebration of the Lord's Supper.

In one group meeting that I led once during Eastertide, I began by leading them in prayer after which I offered a short exposition of the Emmaus Road story. In that story, the disciples proclaim that Jesus "had been made known to them in the breaking of the bread" (Luke 24:35). Having recounted the story, I then asked the servers to share stories from their ministry: "Where have you seen Christ at work?" Sharing such stories can be deeply encouraging. After that, I reviewed nursing home etiquette with them, specifically focusing on NPO ("nothing by mouth") questions (see earlier discussion on page 98). In another meeting with the same group, I reviewed the rubrics about what to do with Communion elements that remain when the visits for the day are completed. This latter came in response to a complaint from a Communion steward who had discovered several returned sets containing unconsumed elements. Although we had covered this issue in their training, periodic review of key points is necessary. Many of us require more than one reminder before we learn a key lesson. Provide review training insistently, regularly, but also gently. Always remember that you are working with volunteers, and you should assume that they mean well.

In addition to problem-solving and reminders, continuing study and reflection on the Eucharist will increase both general understanding of the sacrament and devotion to it. The work of home Communion servers visually reminds the church that mission and Eucharist are connected. As such, this ministry group can be the vanguard for sacramental renewal and mission in the congregation. Cultivate them and work to deepen their devotion to Holy Communion. Others will follow their example.

Administrative Tasks Related to Home Communion Serving

Good record keeping is vital to the life of the church. Otherwise, how will we know where to find the sheep who belong to the sheepfold (John 10:1), and how will we know whether one (or more) of them is lost (Luke 15: 3-7)? Keep baptism and membership rolls up to date, as well as a list of homebound members and a record of visits made to each. Someone should regularly update and review the Communion visitation list, probably on a monthly basis. One is not permanently assigned to the list, as if it were like a prelude to Last Rites. Nor should the church think of their visitation list simply as a list of its elderly members. Many octogenarians and even older persons attend worship quite regularly. Ask the key question: Who is missing? Then listen carefully for the answer. You may need to list younger members recovering from surgery or illness and others whose work schedules may keep them from attending the congregational Eucharist. Announcements posted in the Sunday bulletin, the church newsletter, and the church website can tell people how to request a home Communion visit, although, again, the pastor and congregation should take the initiative and make specific offers to visit those who need it. Remember, it is the shepherd's job to seek the sheep. Ideally, visit people on the list every time Communion is offered, although it may not be possible to maintain that ideal.

Although the pastor or pastoral staff should be consulted about the composition of the visitation list and related visitation records, someone else should maintain them. Churches should not ask their pastors to double as secretaries. Someone within the Communion servers group might serve as visitation captain, or some other well-organized person might assume this administrative role, keeping the records and perhaps making the telephone calls and scheduling the visits. As with good church secretaries and administrative assistants, the visitation captain must understand the common rules about confidentiality and must observe them. Record visits and submit them on the following form, and forward appropriate references to the pastor (see the question at the bottom of the form).

HOME COMMUNION VISITATION REPORT

(Please return to the visitation captain)

Visitation Team: _____

Person(s) visited: _____

Place visited: _____

Date/Time of visit: _____

Did you learn anything that the pastor should know? (Please describe details below and on the reverse side.)

The rubrics and disciplines described in this chapter exist to help the church accomplish its ministry and to safeguard its integrity. Again, it is important that everyone in the church understands his/her own role and exercises it properly, to the end that the ministry of the church be clarified and strengthened. That should occur if these disciplines are kept.

In the next chapter, I will discuss a significant misunderstanding that has arisen in relation to home Communion serving, one that threatens to confuse the meaning and purpose of the Eucharist and thereby threatens to hinder its effectiveness.

Questions and Topics for Discussion

1. Make a list of the ministries of outreach or nurture that your congregation sponsors. Make a list of similar ministries, not directly sponsored by your congregation, in which your members participate. Having made those lists, consider the following:

    - In what specific ways are these ministries and the people who participate in them supported within your congregation's worship? (Through rites of commissioning or blessing? Through occasional prayers offered by the pastor and/or the congregation? Through occasional spoken or multi-media presentations? Through offerings? In some other way?) Please give specific descriptions.
    - Pick one ministry from the list that you have just compiled and compose a short prayer of thanksgiving and intercession that the congregation might offer on its behalf.

2. Obtain a copy of your congregation's home Communion list. Consider the following:

    - What is the procedure for adding persons to this list?
    - Who maintains this list, and how often is it updated? (Are people removed from the list when they no longer need to be on it?)
    - How often are the people visited, and who keeps records of those visits?
    - How could your church improve the system that you have just described?

3. To the extent that you are at liberty to do so, describe a support (or accountability) group of which you have been a member. Consider the following:

- What aspects of the group process were/are helpful for you? What made/makes them helpful?
- What aspects of the group process were/are not as helpful for you? What made/makes them so?
- As you see it, what should a ministry group for home Communion servers seek to accomplish. Be specific. How often should it meet?

Notes

1. Aidan Kavanagh, *Elements of Rite, A Handbook of Liturgical Style* (Collegeville, Minnesota: The Liturgical Press, 1982, 1990), 31.

2. *The United Methodist Book of Worship* (Nashville: The United Methodist Publishing House, 1992), 591-2. Used by permission.

3. *The United Methodist Book of Worship*, 1992, 591. Used by permission.

4. *The United Methodist Book of Worship* 1992, 592. Used by permission.

6

Extension of the Table to Entire Congregations— A Significant Dilemma

In this chapter, I will discuss a practice that has emerged in the years since the United Methodist Church officially restored the practice of sending Holy Communion from the congregational service to the unwillingly absent (1992). Some bishops and district superintendents have concluded that the principles applied to extended table within congregations should be applied to congregations without clergy leadership. A provision that began with the 1996 *Discipline* supports this application. It says, "This distribution also may apply to laypersons who have been assigned pastoral roles in a church or in more than one church by the district superintendent."[1] Missional compassion motivates this form of extended table. Nevertheless, I will argue that sending previously consecrated elements to full congregations is forbidden both in Article XVIII of the Articles of Religion and in "This Holy Mystery," and rightly so. I will describe the dilemma expressed in this practices, and then note some of its unintended consequences. Having done that, I will then suggest more constructive ways to solve the problem.

Describing the Dilemma

As I described earlier, I began seriously reflecting on the work of extending Communion in response to a question posed to me by my district superintendent (see "Introduction," p. 11). He contacted me in the fall of 1994, wanting me to explain "this new practice" of laity taking Communion to shut-ins. Motivated by his question, I trained some members of my congregation and over the next several years led training events in various conference and local-church venues. Various people noticed this developing practice and reflected upon it. I realized that a serious jump in logic had occurred when a new district superintendent asked me if "this thing that you're doing" (i.e., extended table training) could be used to provide Communion for small congregations without a duly authorized pastor. The question took me by surprise. I told him "no," extended table was not intended to cover that need. Nevertheless, I realized that the question emerged for good reasons. Some congregations in his district did not have appointed clergy; Lay Speakers preached and offered minimal pastoral care but could not, of course, preside at Holy Communion. It was a good question. How could these Christians receive the Communion that we say they need?

On a less urgent note, what should congregations that commune weekly do when their pastor goes away on vacation? What should they do to provide Communion for the youth group's weekend retreat? "This Holy Mystery" tells them what they should *not* do. Within its section entitled "The Communion Elements," it says:

> The practice of consecrating elements ahead of time for the convenience of the pastor not having to go to small or remote congregations, weekend camps, or such other cases is inappropriate and contrary to our historic doctrine and understanding of how God's grace is made available in the sacrament (Article XVIII, The Articles of Religion, BOD; page 64). If authorized leadership is not available for celebrating the Lord's Supper, other worship services such as love feasts, agape meals, or baptismal reaffirmations are valid alternatives that avoid the misuse of Communion elements.
>
> The consecrated elements of bread and wine are used for distribution to the sick and others who wish to commune but are unable to attend congregational worship.[2]

As indicated, this conclusion is based on Article XVIII, "Of the Lord's Supper," which says that "The Sacrament of the Lord's Supper was not by Christ's ordinance reserved."[3] Although my superintendent's query came before

"This Holy Mystery" was written, Article XVIII is clear enough. According to the Articles, extension to full congregations is out of order. Nevertheless, many have done so, and the *Discipline* now seems to allow it. Why?

Some simply may not know Article XVIII and its implications. On a deeper level, however, extension to full congregations expresses the missional impulse many Methodists feel. When Methodists perceive a tension between maintaining classic ecclesiastical disciplines, on the one hand, and human need on the other, typically they will adjust ecclesiology to fulfill the need. They bend ecclesiology to the shape of the mission. Liturgical exceptions have been permitted, if not encouraged. Thus, John Wesley went into the parishes of other priests and preached in the fields, and later he ordained elders for America, although Anglican canon law forbade both. In the late nineteenth century, American Methodists began using grape juice at the Lord's Supper, forsaking the normative Christian tradition of wine for the sake of its temperance witness. Recently, the United Methodist Church has said that seekers may receive Communion prior to baptism, thus making an exception to the classic sacramental *ordo*.[4] Flexibility in service of mission is generally a good thing, but such moves have complicated our ecumenical relationships, and they can lead to negative consequences.[5] Because it is part of their tradition, Methodists will most likely continue to make sacramental and liturgical exceptions, but they should not make them in a haphazard manner. They should determine if there are more traditional ways to address perceived needs.

The dilemma that I describe in this chapter is, of course, a real one. In the following commentary, United Methodist layman James Lane expresses the key issues:

> The United Methodist Church emphasizes Communion not only as a meal of grace, but a meal of grace that is open to all.
>
> In 2004, the General Conference of the United Methodist Church adopted the document "A Response to This Holy Mystery: A United Methodist Understanding of Holy Communion." We said: "In accord with the practice of the church throughout Christian history, God calls and the church sets apart certain persons for leadership within the body of Christians. We believe that the Holy Spirit gives to such persons the grace and gifts they need for leadership in obedience to their call. Elders are ordained to a lifetime ministry of service, word, sacrament, and order" (*Book of Discipline*, Paragraph 323) and charged to "administer the sacraments of baptism and the Lord's Supper and all the other means of grace" (Paragraph 331).
>
> On a recent Sunday, I was asked to be responsible for the entire service at our church, including the sermon. Our pastor was to be away that day.

We are a church that serves communion every Sunday. I am a layperson and am not authorized, according to the *Discipline* of our church, to consecrate the elements. What were we to do? We wanted to continue our practice, so our pastor consecrated the elements earlier in the week before she left. Lay people in our denomination are allowed to serve the elements once they have been properly consecrated.

My sermon topic that day was "Touchstones of Life." I talked about the touchstones from my growing-up years and some of those in my adult life . . . .

As I came to [the end of my sermon], I walked to the table on which our Communion elements had been prepared.

I then explained that Jesus left us with a "Touchstone of Life" by saying these words:

"Take this bread, take this cup. As often as you do this, do it in remembrance of me."

I uncovered the elements, broke the bread and lifted the cup. I then shared these old and familiar words with our congregation:

"You that do truly and earnestly repent of your sins, and are in love and charity with your neighbors and intend to lead a new life, following the commandments of God, and walking from henceforth in his holy ways, draw near with faith, and take this holy sacrament to your comfort."

"We do not presume to come to this thy table, O merciful Lord, trusting in our own righteousness, but in thy manifold and great mercies. We are not worthy so much as to gather up the crumbs under thy table. But, thou art the same Lord, whose property is always to have mercy. Grant us therefore, gracious Lord, so to partake of this sacrament of thy Son Jesus Christ that we may walk in newness of life, may grow into his likeness and may evermore dwell in him, and he in us. Amen."

And then as a remembrance of what Jesus Christ has done for us and continues to do for us, we shared the bread and cup of life with each other . . . .

When our history is being written, what will it say of how we lived out the command to take and eat, take and drink, in remembrance of the one who offered up himself?

Will it say that we so often missed out on this "meal of healing and grace" because a person of the right pedigree and with proper credentials was not present to lead us? Will we be "law" filled or "grace" filled?

God grant that we lead with a grace-filled access to all that is holy![6]

There is much to affirm in Mr. Lane's commentary, especially the understanding of Holy Communion as a means of grace along with the affirmation of "constant Communion." His congregation listened to a primary teaching of "This Holy Mystery" and is offering the sacrament on every Lord's Day.

Moreover, they understand that the church does not grind to a halt when its clergy are absent, another important insight with roots in early Methodism. Indeed, then, their use of previously consecrated elements expresses key Methodist values, yet it contradicts others. How does one resolve the dilemma?

In the remainder of this chapter, I will address two questions. First, what is the problem with extending the table to full congregations? Second, are there better, more constructive ways to respond to such needs?

What Is the Problem? Examining the Unintended Consequences

The gospel encourages Christians to suspect legalism. We need look no further than the controversies about sabbath-keeping between Jesus and the religious authorities of his day. Should the commandment to "remember the sabbath day and keep it holy" (Exodus 20:8) prevent hungry disciples from harvesting a few grains of wheat for their own nourishment (Mark 2: 23-28) or healing a man with a withered hand (Mark 3:1-6)? Jesus said no, "the sabbath was made for humankind, and not humankind for the sabbath" (Mark 2:28) and that it was lawful to do good on the sabbath (Mark 3: 4). At no point, however, does Jesus say that sabbath-keeping is a bad idea that should be rejected. Legalism is the problem—laws and rules as ends in themselves—but not law itself. Some Christians have misunderstood this distinction between law and legalism and thus have come to disregard much classical guidance and systems of discipline. The error is known as antinomianism (literally "against law"). Christians in America may be particularly vulnerable to this misreading of the gospel tradition, given our national heritage of individualism. Lane's discussion of "pedigree" and "proper credentials" reflects this tendency. The suspicion of legalism, coupled with antinomianism, affects our reading of liturgical rubrics.

As I have discussed elsewhere, during the late Middle Ages, rubrics that limited presiding at the Lord's Supper to presbyters (i.e., to priests and elders) were practiced in a less-than-pastoral manner, sometimes making Communion into the private experience of the ordained. Even today, some clergy (both Protestants and Catholics) will speak of the Eucharist as if it somehow belongs to them and not to the church. Nevertheless, the problem is not with the rubric, but with its faulty application. Reform has occurred (and is occurring), and so we retain the tradition of clergy presiders, but we insist that presiding at Table is something that they do in relation to the assembly. The rubrics exist to encourage that gathering. Liturgical theologian

Aidan Kavanagh has suggested that we understand rubrics as "liturgical proverbs," as wisdom that the church has preserved and given to us.[7] Understood thus, classic rubrics deserve careful reflection. Before discarding them because they present certain challenges, we should meditate upon them, allowing them to reveal their wisdom. Viewed in this manner, the clergy rule is quite liberating. It forces the assembly to gather and sets each order—laity, deacons, and elders—free to do its particular work.

The rule against extending Communion to entire congregations preserves the important link between the Communion liturgy and receiving Communion itself. That is its wisdom. As I described in chapter two, in the earliest days of the church, the faithful experienced the Lord's Day liturgy as one event that involved gathering, hearing the word, offerings, prayer of thanksgiving, and Communion. Sending Communion to the unwillingly absent placed a short temporal and spatial gap between the community's thanksgiving and the Communion of those absent members, but the gap was not theologically significant. They understood Communion within and beyond the assembly as one act of serving within one gathering. As we discussed earlier, the gap between thanksgiving and Communion widened considerably over the centuries, until Catholic practice in the late Middle Ages included numerous celebrations of the mass, but only annual Communion for most church members. Reform came slowly. At the behest of Pope Pius X early in the twentieth century, Catholics began communing more often, but not always as part of the mass itself. With the Eucharist seen primarily as an action of the clergy, large numbers of communicants could be an inconvenience. Odd as it may seem to us now, it was not unusual for people to receive Communion from the reserved sacrament after the conclusion of mass, and sometimes before it.[8] Scholars and theologians formed by the Liturgical Movement have worked hard to overcome this split between liturgy and Communion.

As a means of overcoming that split, we have come to understand that we encounter Christ's presence through the unfolding of the entire liturgy—gathering, praising God, hearing and responding to the Word, confessing sin and making peace, offering and giving thanks, receiving Communion, and going forth in mission. Communities can retain a eucharistic shape when they engage in the full liturgy and extend Communion to some individuals who are unable to gather with it; indeed, such extension encourages the missional character of the whole. A Christian community can hardly retain its eucharistic shape, however, if it never enacts the full liturgy.[9]

It may be helpful for United Methodists to realize that our Catholic sisters and brothers also face the problem of congregations without priests. Contemporary Catholics have listened to the teachings of their church, and members have come to expect Communion on a frequent, weekly basis, but priests are in short supply. This coincidence of trends causes a problem. To address it, the church developed orders for "Sunday Worship in the Absence of a Priest" (SWAP), in which Lay Eucharistic Ministers carry Communion to full congregations. Originally, their work had been limited to serving Communion to persons in private homes, nursing homes, and hospitals, but it was expanded, and with less than happy results. In his book, *The Dilemma of Priestless Sundays*, Catholic theologian James Dallen insists that focus on the consecrated elements themselves, perhaps inevitable with SWAP, stifles mission and perpetuates the understanding of the Eucharist as a private devotional act.[10]

What should be done? Since Sunday and the Eucharist are a dynamic pair, Dallen insists that Catholics should find a way to ordain the leaders of congregations.[11] He argues that congregations not only have a "right" to the Eucharist, but they have a duty to offer it,[12] that is, they are called to engage in the full liturgy. Here Methodists will hear an echo of John Wesley's teaching that "constant Communion" is our "duty."[13] As we have already described, when Wesley and members of the Church of England spoke of "Communion," the implied the eucharistic gathering of the full community and not just the receiving of consecrated elements. Again, the church is called to Eucharist, and the Eucharist forms the church for mission. Dallen's caution applies directly to United Methodists. We need to guard against the idea that Communion consists primarily in receiving one's share of the consecrated matter.

Scholarly honesty requires that I point to a fifth-century Roman practice known as the *fermentum*, which provides an intriguing ritual precedent to the practice of extending the table to full congregations. On the Lord's Day, the Pope would celebrate mass in one of the churches in the city. As a sign of unity, he would then send fragments of consecrated bread to other churches in the city. A fragment was placed in the chalice of each congregation. Scholars have long assumed that the presbyter within each congregation then proceeded to make an additional offering of the Eucharist, but John Baldovin has recently challenged this idea, suggesting "the *fermentum* served not only for the presbyter's Communion but for the faithful who were gathered in the titular church."[14] The fragment was believed to affect what Baldovin calls "consecration by contact,"[15] with the small, consecrated piece, as it were, extending the work of consecration to the previously unconsecrated matter. According to Baldovin's reading, there was one Eucharist, and then congregations throughout the city received Communion from that one celebration, a practice that seems not unlike the contemporary SWAP and the United Methodist provision that we have noted.[16] Should we use this ancient precedent as a justification for extending of the Table to a full congregation? Baldovin says not:

> The situation of fifth-century Rome should *not* be used to argue for the acceptability of Sunday communion services without the full celebration of the Eucharist. It would be impossible for us today to recapture the sense of unity among Roman Christians. Recent Roman Catholic documents have re-emphasized the importance of receiving communion from the bread and wine consecrated at the local Sunday celebration.[17]

One can make a similar argument based on United Methodist liturgical texts and official documents.

We should reject a simple one-to-one correspondence between precedent and current practices for two primary reasons: (1) As Baldovin argues, our current practice exists for reasons other than that which drove the fifth-century Roman practice—theirs was an expression of unity; SWAP and extension to full congregations is an attempt to solve the ecclesial dilemma caused by a shortage of clergy. (2) We believe that the current practice of communing the whole congregation from bread and wine consecrated in their midst is the ideal practice, whether or not that was widespread practice in every corner of the ancient church. Wisdom respects precedent. Nevertheless, practices are retained not simply because they are venerable, but because we believe them to be true.

Extension of Communion to full congregations can encourage the unfortunate understanding of elders as those empowered to speak the "magic words" of consecration and thus confect the sacrament. As I have stated elsewhere, the United Methodist form for the Great Thanksgiving allows no such understanding, but instead calls for pastor and congregation to speak in dialogue. While there is one primary voice—that of the pastor—the great "Amen," which belongs to the congregation, indicates that the whole community offers the prayer, including the Words of Institution and the epiclesis.[18] The unfortunate notion that clergy do sacramental magic can undermine faithful discipleship among the laity and encourage clergy to hold an immature, controlling view of their office. The church is better off, therefore, when it allows extension of the table to be the relatively modest action that was perceived when "A Service of Word and Table V" was first approved and published. That is, laypersons serve the unwillingly absent members of the congregation with Communion sent directly from the Sunday worship service. Such work fulfills a particular pastoral need with liturgical and theological integrity. That is enough.

What, then, do we tell congregations that find themselves without regular pastoral leadership and thus cannot celebrate Holy Communion on a regular basis? What do we tell their district superintendents who attempt to secure adequate leadership for them but struggle to do so within the provisions of the existing *Discipline* and ritual? I will address this question in the next section.

Constructive Responses to the Problem

Extending the table, modestly understood, is an attempt to include an unwillingly absent member within the assembly. The process involves representative members of the local church taking the elements to them and sharing fellowship. Consecrating bread and wine ahead of time and sending it to other churches turns Communion primarily into a thing and not a gathering that handles holy things.[19]

Perhaps we are facing the unintended consequence of the introduction and subsequent strengthening of the epiclesis within our Great Thanksgivings. *Epiclesis*, a Greek work which means, literally, "to call upon," is the petition in the Great Thanksgiving in which the church invokes the presence of the Holy Spirit, calling upon God to make the sacrament effective in our midst.[20] Including an epiclesis in our eucharistic prayers is a relatively new practice for American Methodists. The first *Book of Common Prayer*, published in 1549, had included the following epiclesis in its eucharistic prayer.

> Hear us (O merciful father) we beseech thee; and with thy holy spirit and word, vouchsafe to blesse and sanctifie these thy gifts, and creatures of bread and wine, that they may be unto us the body and blood of thy most dearly beloved son Jesus Christ.[21]

Rubrics called for the priest to make the sign of the cross over the elements at the words "blesse" and "sanctifie." Some argued, however, that people could too easily interpret the prayer as supporting transubstantiation, and thus it was removed in the 1552 revision of the prayerbook. There was no epiclesis in the 1662 *Book of Common Prayer*, the version in use during John

Wesley's ministry, nor was one included in *The Sunday Service for the Methodists in North America*. This usage remained through publication of the eucharistic rite in *The Book of Hymns* (1966). Shortly thereafter, however, liturgical scholarship related to the post-Vatican II reforms asserted that an epiclesis was included in many ancient eucharistic prayers, the so-called *Apostolic Tradition* (attributed to Hippolytus) being a prime example.[22] An emerging generation of United Methodist reformers was following this scholarship, and contributing to it as well, and so *The Sacrament of the Lord's Supper, An Alternate Text* (published in 1972) included the following epiclesis:

> Send the power of Your Holy Spirit on us,
>> gathered here out of love for you,
>> and on these gifts.
>
> Help us know
>> in the breaking of the bread
>> and the drinking of this wine
>> the presence of Christ
>> who gave his body and blood for mankind.
>
> Make us one with Christ,
>> one with each other,
>> and one in service to all mankind.[23]

Some considered this version of the epiclesis a weak first attempt, arguing that the petition lacked theological and linguistic clarity.[24] What did "Help us know" mean? Positively speaking, the 1972 epiclesis exhibits what we might call a Lukan sense of presence, that is, of Christ known to the faithful in the breaking of the bread (Luke 24:35), in the midst of the liturgical community. As I have demonstrated, much of the argument of the liturgical movement has moved in this direction, focusing on Christ's presence in community. Nevertheless, historical experience suggests that a Johannine (or Markan) sense of Christ's presence located in the bread itself is necessary to the formation of a more serious eucharistic piety; certainly, that has been the assumption in the Christian West. The version of the epiclesis that emerged at the end of the United Methodist revision process reflects these latter sensibilities. It reads as follows:

> Pour out your Holy Spirit on us gathered here,
>> and on these gifts of bread and wine.
>
> Make them be for us the body and blood of Christ,
>> that we may be for the world the body of Christ,
>> redeemed by his blood.[25]

Unmistakably it calls for a change in the bread and wine, although exactly how we understand that change remains open to interpretation. The church has been using this strong epiclesis since the General Conference of 1984 approved and included it in *The Book of Services*, published in 1985.[26] It gained widespread circulation and usage with the publication of *The United Methodist Hymnal* in 1989. Again, it is a clear and strongly worded text, one that calls for a change in the elements themselves: "Make them be for us the body and blood of Christ."[27] After more than two decades of use, should we be surprised, then, that these words have formed people, that they have heard them and taken them seriously? Should we be surprised when people come to believe that God does, in fact, work a change in the elements? Shaped by this strong epiclesis, some may be willing to practice something more than simple extension within the congregation, that is, something like reservation or extension to full congregations. Our text has encouraged this possibility.

Appropriating the words of the 1972 epiclesis and combining them with our current form would further reshape our understanding. We could do so without surrendering the theological strength expressed in the current form. Thus, we would pray our epiclesis in the following manner:

Pour out your Holy Spirit on us gathered here,
    and on these gifts of bread and wine.

Make them be for us the body and blood of Christ,
    that we may be for the world the body of Christ,
    redeemed by his blood.[28]

Help us know
    in the breaking of the bread
    and the drinking of this wine
    the presence of Christ
    who gave his body and blood for all.[29]

Adding of the "help us know" petition is fully permissible according to the rubrics of *The United Methodist Book of Worship*, which allow for the addition of appropriate text at the places in "A Service of Word and Table II" that are marked by the asterisk (*). One such place is the epiclesis, at which point one could add the 1972 petition.[30] There exists a significant Anglican precedent for such a doubling of phrases. In *The Book of Common Prayer* (1549), the words of delivery for the Communion bread said, "The body of our Lord Jesus Christ which was given for thee, preserve thy body and soul unto everlasting life."[31] Like the 1549 epiclesis, that form was critiqued as overly Catholic and was replaced by the following form in the 1552 book: "Take and eat this, in remembrance that Christ died for thee, and feed on him in thy heart by faith, with thanksgiving."[32] That phrase, in turn, was perceived as a Protestant overreaction to the idea of objective grace present in the elements themselves. What could be done? As a peacemaking gesture, the 1559 prayerbook combined the two phrases, providing the comprehensive words of delivery that are still used in many Anglican liturgies. They were the words of delivery in American Methodist rites until the recent revisions, and they remain as part of "A Service of Word and Table IV."

> The Body of our Lord Jesus Christ,
> which was given for thee,
> preserve thy soul and body unto everlasting life.

> Take and eat this
> in remembrance that Christ died for thee,
> and feed on him in thy heart
> by faith with thanksgiving.[33]

So, expanding our epiclesis might profit our eucharistic piety in a more liturgical/communitarian fashion without losing other important gains in that piety. But, the question remains. What shall we do if we decide that extension of the table to full congregations is inappropriate, as I am arguing? Shall we simply close those churches or tell them that they cannot have the Eucharist? Indeed, closing some local churches might be a wise option, especially when we are staffing multiple small congregations in the same general area. Providing pastoral coverage for an area might also be worked out in cooperation with our ecumenical partners—it is not necessary that there be a *United Methodist* congregation in every locale. Nevertheless, closure must not be abandonment of ministry, an unthinkable option for Wesleyans.

How then can remote United Methodist parishes receive the Lord's Supper? Solving the problem in the long run may require some adjustments in our ecclesiology, including questions about why we have clergy in the first place. In some places, it seems that we have too many clergy and in other places too few. Most Sundays, I attend church at a large urban congregation that sits on the corner of our Southern Methodist University campus, a congregation that currently sponsors nine full worship services every Lord's Day, and that number may continue to increase. We need plenty of leadership and indeed we have it. Between the church staff and the various ordained university persons who attend, some Sundays it seems that we have enough clergy on hand to staff a small diocese. Then, I hear reports about regions in the southwestern United States that have no United Methodist clergy, ordained or otherwise, for hundreds of miles. So then, how many clergy are needed? The question is not simply answered. It would seem, however, that the church's willingness to maintain a congregation in a particular locale implies an obligation to provide them with authorized pastoral leadership who can lead a full Eucharist at regular intervals. If we say that this celebration should occur every Lord's Day, then theoretically such leadership should be available to them every Sunday. Of course, American Methodists have come to see various other Communion schedules as normal—quarterly and monthly Communion being two well-known examples. I will reluctantly concede that some congregations may have to adjust to one of these less frequent schedules, at least for a time.

However, the pastoral needs of congregations and other religious communities should shape the rules for authorizing clergy leadership.[34] For instance, a former parishioner of mine, a certified lay speaker, has been *de facto* the pastor of a small congregation in a nearby city for many years. He has handled the preaching, but has had to make other arrangements to provide for their sacramental needs—at times, asking pastors from neighboring congregations to preside at Table and yes at times taking previously consecrated elements to his service. If he is able to preach regularly without benefit of ordination (or local pastor's license), then why not grant him some sort of limited license to administer the sacraments? In many ways, effective preaching requires more theological discernment than administration of the sacraments, and we seem to have little problem with allowing some lay speakers to preach on a regular basis. Why this allowance and not the other? Some have argued that we should revive the office of local elder, which would allow the church to ordain such people and allow them to function in one particular congregation.[35] There would be no need for annual conference membership to accompany such ordination. Such persons would be appointed as needed and would otherwise not exercise the sacramental role of an elder. Catholics already understand such distinctions—priests who enter holy matrimony do not cease to be priests, even though they normally give up priestly functions.

Such licensing—or even ordaining—may represent something more radical than the church is willing to embrace at this point, and it would require changes in *The Book of Discipline*. A proper supervisory and mentoring system would be necessary, but that could be arranged.[36] In the meantime, as the *Discipline* directs, properly credentialed clergy serving in extension ministries might be employed to meet some of this need. It states:

All conference members who are elders in full connection, including those in extension ministries, shall be available and on call to administer the sacraments of baptism and the Lord's Supper as required by the *Discipline* (¶ 340.2a) and requested by the district superintendent of the district in which the appointment is held.[37]

I point to this provision with a certain amount of fear. If I were asked to serve under it, would I have time to do my work as a professor? But I also make it knowing that I have served over eight years as an extension minister and have filed reports with local district superintendents each year, and I have never been called—not once—to help a congregation that does not have adequate leadership for the Lord's Supper. Other colleagues with longer service in extension ministry have a similar testimony, to their regret in many cases. I do help frequently in my local church and in other congregations when asked, as do many of my extension colleagues.

What else could be done? Something like the Quarterly Conference revivals held in late eighteenth and early nineteenth-century American Methodism might be held in some of the remote regions, in which people would be asked to come together for regional Communion festivals.[38] If I and other extension ministers were asked to offer such service once or twice a year, we might at least begin to address the problem. We are missing an opportunity here.

Questions and Topics for Discussion

1. What happens in the Sunday service of your local church when the pastor is absent? Is Holy Communion offered on those days, or is it omitted? If it is offered, how is it done on those Sundays? Are retired clergy or clergy on extension appointments invited to help?

2. Does your church offer Communion at any of its out-of-town retreats? How is this handled? How might this practice be improved? (Are there clergy available who might be invited to attend or visit the retreat?)

3. Review the perspective expressed by James Lane in the opinion piece provided on pages 105-106. With what parts of his argument do you agree or disagree? Can you describe another way that his congregation could have responded to the dilemma they were facing?

4. Do you think that extending the table to entire congregations is a problem? Why or why not? How would you address the problem of congregations without authorized sacramental leadership?

Notes

1. From *The Book of Discipline of the United Methodist Church, 1996*, ¶1115.9. Copyright © 1996 by the United Methodist Publishing House. Used by permission.

See also *The Book of Discipline of the United Methodist Church, 2004* (Nashville: The United Methodist Publishing House, 2004), ¶1117.9.

2. "This Holy Mystery, A United Methodist Understanding of Holy Communion," *The Book of Resolutions of the United Methodist Church*, 2004, page 921-22. Copyright © 2004, The United Methodist Publishing House, used by permission.

3. *The Book of Discipline of the United Methodist Church, 2004*, ¶ 103, 64. Used by permission.

4. I discuss this category of the sacramental and liturgical exception in my book, *Let Every Soul Be Jesus' Guest, A Theology of the Open Table* (Nashville: Abingdon Press, 2006), chapter 2, 19-40.

5. For instance, what will become of mutual recognition of ordained ministries between the Episcopal Church and the United Methodist Church if the latter also allows Licensed Local Pastors—that is, non-ordained lay pastors—to preside at the Lord's Table.?

6. "Commentary: Finding the Holy Grail at the Communion Table." A United Methodist News (UMNS) commentary by James Lane. December 11, 2006. Reprinted courtesy of United Methodist News Service. <http://www.umc.org/site/c.gjJTJbMUIuE/b.2286623/k.B624/Commentary_Finding_the_Holy_Grail_at_the_communion_table.htm>.

Accessed June 22, 2007.

"You that do truly . . ." is a slight adaptation of the classical sixteenth-century *Book of Common Prayer* invitation. It remains in United Methodist rites as part of "A Service of Word and Table IV," *The United Methodist Hymnal* (Nashville: The United Methodist Publishing House, 1989), 26-31, especially page 26. "We do not presume" is the classic Anglican (and Methodist) "Prayer of Humble Access" from the same sources, specifically page 30 of *UMH*.

The title of the General Conference resolution is incorrectly noted. It is "This Holy Mystery," etc.; and not "A Response to This Holy Mystery."

7. Aidan Kavanagh, *Elements of Rite, A Handbook of Liturgical Style* (A Pueblo Book. Collegeville, MN: The Liturgical Press, 1982, 1990), 8. Copyright © 1982, 1990, by The Order of Saint Benedict, Inc. Published by Liturgical Press, Collegeville, MN. Reprinted with permission.

8. Nathan Mitchell, *Cult and Controversy: The Worship of the Eucharist Outside Mass* (A Pueblo Book. Collegeville, MN: The Liturgical Press, 1982, 1990), 228.

9. Indeed, in the case of those who are permanently unable to gather with the full congregation, regular practice of extended table Communion might well be supplemented from time to time by an extended congregation (that is, at least five or six church members plus an elder) so that long-term shut-ins can occasionally experience the full eucharistic action.

10. James Dallen, Foreword by Bishop William E. McManus, *The Dilemma of Priestless Sundays* (Chicago: Liturgy Training Publications, 1994), 104.

11. Ibid., 138.

12. Ibid., 137.

13. John Wesley, "The Duty of Constant Communion," *The Works of John Wesley,* Volume 7 (Grand Rapids, Michigan: Zondervan Publishing House, produced from an 1872 edition), 147.

14. John F. Baldovin, "The *Fermentum* at Rome in the Fifth Century: A Reconsideration," *Worship* 79:1 (January 2005), 47. Used by permission.

15. Ibid.

16. Ibid., 51. *The Book of Discipline of the United Methodist Church, 2004* (Nashville: The United Methodist Church, 2004), ¶1117.9.

17. John F. Baldovin, "The *Fermentum* at Rome in the Fifth Century: A Reconsideration," 53.

18. Mark W. Stamm, *Sacraments and Discipleship* (Nashville: Discipleship Resources, 2001), 92-104.

19. Eduard Schillebeeckx, *Christ the Sacrament of the Encounter with God* (Kansas City, MO: Sheed and Ward, 1963), 44.

20. See my discussion of the epiclesis in *Sacraments and Discipleship*, 99-104.

21. *The Book of Common Prayer*, 1549. <http://justus.anglican.org/resources/bcp/1549/Communion_1549.htm>. Accessed June 28, 2007.

22. R.C.D. Jasper and G.J. Cuming, *Prayers of the Eucharist, Early and Reformed* (Collegeville, Minnesota: The Liturgical Press, 1975, 1980, 1990), 33.

23. *The Sacrament of the Lord's Supper, An Alternate Text. Music Edition* (Nashville: The Methodist Publishing House, 1972), from "Sacrament of the Lord's Supper (Alternate Text) Music Edition" ©1972, 1975 The United Methodist Publishing House. Used by permission.

24. For a description of the general strengthening of the epiclesis over the period from 1970 until 1984, see Robert Brian Peiffer, *How Contemporary Liturgies Evolve: The Revision of United Methodist Liturgical Texts (1968-1988)* (Unpublished Ph.D. dissertation, University of Notre Dame, 1993), 30.

See also Hoyt L. Hickman, "Word and Table: The Process of Liturgical Revision in the United Methodist Church, 1964-1992," "*The Sunday Service of the Methodists, Twentieth-Century Worship in Worldwide Methodism. Studies in Honor of James F. White.* Edited by Karen B. Westerfield Tucker (Nashville: Kingswood Books, 1996), 117-35.

25. *The United Methodist Hymnal* (Nashville: The United Methodist Publishing House, 1989), 10. From "A Service of Word and Table I" © 1972, 1980, 1985, 1989, The United Methodist Publishing House. Used by permission.

26. *The Book of Services, Containing the General Services of the Church Adopted*

by the 1984 General Conference, the United Methodist Church (Nashville: The United Methodist Publishing House, 1985), 24-25.

27. *The United Methodist Hymnal*, 1989, 10. Used by permission.

28. Ibid. Used by permission.

29. *The Sacrament of the Lord's Supper, An Alternate Text. Music Edition* (Nashville: The Methodist Publishing House, 1972), 17. In the updating, I have substituted the word "all" for "mankind." From "Sacrament of the Lord's Supper (Alternate Text) Music Edition" ©1972, 1975 The United Methodist Publishing House. Used by permission.

30. *The United Methodist Book of Worship* (Nashville: The United Methodist Publishing House, 1992), 40. Compare *The United Methodist Hymnal*, 1989, 14.

31. *The Book of Common Prayer,* 1549. <http://justus.anglican.org/resources/bcp/1549/Communion_1549.htm>. Accessed June 28, 2007.

32. *The Book of Common Prayer,* 1552. <http://justus.anglican.org/resources/bcp/1552/Communion_1552.htm>. Accessed June 28, 2007.

33. *The United Methodist Hymnal* (Nashville: The United Methodist Publishing House, 1989), 31. Compare *The Book of Common Prayer*, 1979, 338. From "A Service of Word and Table IV" ©1957 Board of Publication, Evangelical United Brethren Church; ©1964, 1965, 1989 The United Methodist Publishing House. Used by permission.

Notice that *The United Methodist Hymnal* version reverses the order of the words "soul" and "body."

34. I am not arguing for a rigid definition of congregation. For instance, seminary communities are not congregations in the strict sense, but they do engage in regular worship, sometimes on a daily basis. Thus, some faculty members should be ordained, including career academics. Historically, Methodism has not defined itself simply as a collection of local churches, nor should we think of there being a sharp distinction between pastoral and academic work.

35. See article by Ted A. Campbell, "The Oral Roberts Option: The Case for Ordained Local Elders (and Local Deacons?) in the United Methodist Church" *Quarterly Review* 24:4 (Winter 2004), 358-66.

36. Many of these issues were discussed in "Minutes of Several Conversations Between the Study of Ministry Commission, Chairs of the Orders and Boards of Ordained Ministry of Annual Conferences, Various Laity and Clergy across the Connection, and the General Conference of The United Methodist Church," a report considered by the 2008 General Conference.

37. From *The Book of Discipline of the United Methodist Church, 2004*, ¶ 344.3, p. 247. Copyright © 2004 by the United Methodist Publishing House. Used by permission.

38. Russell E. Richey, *The Methodist Conference in America, A History* (Nashville: Kingswood Books, 1996), 59-61.

For a description of such festivals, see Lester Ruth, *A Little Heaven Below, Worship at Early Methodist Quarterly Meetings* (Nashville: Abingdon Press, 2000), 103-155.

7

Ten Important Questions

I have trained various groups of home Communion servers over the years, both in local congregations and in regional gatherings. I begin the process by gathering and recording their questions, which I then promise to address during our time together. Taking their questions functions as an icebreaker and usually establishes a positive tone within the class; every question is important.

Their questions are often predictable ones that I address in the normal course of the standard presentations. For example, I usually receive queries about the role of the pastor in relation to laypersons. Occasionally, however, a new issue arises or someone raises an old question with particular vehemence. Whether predictable or not, the questions sharpen my thinking and usually lead to deeper levels of interaction among us. Thus, I have continued asking them, and my lesson plan for each training event allows a block of time to address unanticipated questions. In like manner, I hope that you will consider engaging your colleagues and me with questions that I have not addressed in this book. The conversation is never closed.

In this final chapter, I present a sampling of the most significant questions that I have received over the years, offering a short response to each. Each question presented here represents one that was actually made in a training seminar, although some are composites. These questions and responses function as a summary to this book.

FIRST QUESTION: WHAT IS THE PASTOR'S ROLE IN THE LORD'S SUPPER, AND WHY DO WE HAVE SUCH RUBRICS?

The pastor presides at the Lord's Supper. She or he stands at the altar and makes final preparations for the meal, perhaps receiving elements brought forward in a procession or simply uncovering elements already placed there. When all is prepared, he or she addresses the congregation with the opening line of the *sursum corda*, "The Lord be with you," and the congregation responds, "And also with you."[1] Then, together pastor and congregation move through the prayer. The pastor speaks most of the Great Thanksgiving, but not all of it; the congregation's "Amen" is essential. When the prayer is completed, the pastor breaks the bread and begins serving the people, and others assist him or her in the serving. Hopefully, the pastor receives the bread and cup from the hand of another because clergy, also, are sinners who need to receive God's gift. Receiving from another person embodies such dependence and mutual care; it reminds the church that the pastor remains one of the baptized.[2]

According to the classic tradition, local churches may not celebrate the Eucharist without an elder (or other authorized minister) presiding, and, conversely, pastors may not celebrate the Eucharist without a congregation. Why does the church have such rules? Did the clergy invent them to augment their power? No. Rather, these rules protect the integrity of the Eucharist as a corporate gathering of the church, and they prevent it from becoming a private devotion for the spiritually elite. Persons must "wait for one another" (see 1 Corinthians 11:33) before they begin. Pastors are charged with convening the church and with encouraging it to gather, although regrettably such gathering is never perfectly accomplished. As convener, therefore, the pastor must continue to ask the question, "Who is missing?" and he or she must encourage outreach that moves the church toward a more complete gathering. Home Communion serving is one such effort.

Doubtless, rubrics about the pastoral leadership at the Lord's Supper have been abused, but that does not mean that we should reject them. They express important wisdom. As liturgical theologian Aidan Kavanagh contends, classic rubrics are "liturgical proverbs."[3] We do well to consider them prayerfully and to observe them.

Second Question: What If Someone Challenges Me, Asking, "As a Lay Person, Are You Authorized to Serve Communion?"

You may respond by gently pointing them to the rubric in *The United Methodist Book of Worship*, which says, "The pastor, or laypersons at the direction of the pastor, may distribute the consecrated bread and cup to sick or homebound persons as soon as possible following a service of Word and Table as an extension of that service."[4] You could also show them *The Book of Discipline*, which contains a similar provision.[5] One might also respond, "Yes, our pastor and congregation have sent me, and they told me to come serve you." So yes, if you are trained and sent, then you are authorized to perform this ministry. Even if authorized, however, home Communion servers should not try to force people to receive their ministry.

I have found that questions about the role of the pastor are sometimes lurking within such queries about the propriety of lay servers, including veiled accusations about shirked responsibility and even laziness. However, most of the clergy that I know are hard workers; indeed, many work too hard and should be encouraged to take more time for rest and reflection. So if you find your pastor at the ballpark on a weekday afternoon, you should tell him that you're proud of him for taking care of himself. Furthermore, we need increased clarity about the pastor's role in the local church. On the one hand, pastors need to be acquainted with their parishioners, so it is important that they do some visiting within their congregation. Forming a home Communion servers' ministry does not mean that pastors will cease visiting their homebound members. This intention should be communicated clearly. On the other hand, pastors and other leaders are called "to equip the saints for the work of ministry, to build up the body of Christ" (Ephesians 4:12). They are called to share the blessings of ministry and to help others move toward deeper maturity through active Christian service. That is another reason why persons other than the pastor need to be involved in serving Communion.

Third Question: What Is the Difference Between Extended Table and Reserved Sacrament?

In an extended table Communion, people first attend a congregation's regularly scheduled service and participate in its Communion. Then, they take elements consecrated in that service directly to an absent member of that congregation and serve him or her. Although there is a slight time gap between the Communion given in the primary gathering and that given in the home, we understand that the homebound person is essentially participating in the same Communion service. In the primary gathering, servers would normally carry Communion to the pew or chair of a person who was unable to get up and walk to the chancel rail. In an extended table Communion, we can say that the servers merely carry that Communion several miles further.

In a reserved sacrament, on the other hand, a congregation intentionally consecrates extra elements—usually wafers only, but sometimes wine as well—and stores them in a locked cabinet called a tabernacle. As they are needed in the days following, the elements are retrieved from the tabernacle and used to commune homebound or hospitalized members. In addition, they are used for *viaticum*, that is, for Communion of the dying. In some cases, they are used to provide Communion for congregations without clergy leadership. With reserved sacrament, it is not necessary that reception of the Communion be directly linked to any particular Lord's Day service. So there are clear similarities between extension and reservation, but also marked differences.

United Methodists practice extended table, but not reserved sacrament. They make the distinction for reasons rooted both in their history and in contemporary liturgical theology. In the late Middle Ages, reception of Communion declined sharply while devotion to Christ's presence in the elements, including the reserved host, increased. Various devotional practices developed, particularly public processions of the host and rituals of adoration. The Protestant reformers rejected such practices, primarily because they seemed to ignore Jesus' commandments to eat and drink (Matthew 26: 26-27; 1 Corinthians 11:23-26). This rejection was expressed in the Articles of Religion that were formulated within the sixteenth-century Church of England and then inherited by the Methodist movement. They are retained in our *Discipline*, with Article XVI "Of the Sacraments" specifically forbidding reservation. Thus, inherited United Methodist doctrinal standards forbid reservation, but our rejection of it is based on broader ecumenical concerns. Based on the most ancient precedent, most contemporary liturgical theologians argue that a complete eucharistic celebration involves the gathering of a congregation, reading and preaching of the Word, intercessions, confession and pardon, passing of the peace, Great Thanksgiving, and Communion of the full congregation. Using reserved sacrament encourages too great a separation between the action of the congregation and the reception of Communion.

Fourth Question: How Does One Prepare to Lead a Communion Visit?

Preparing to lead a home Communion visit is not unlike preparing for other liturgical leadership tasks. One's spiritual preparation is vitally important, so home Communion servers should be regular worshipers, people who pray, and people who listen to God and to one another. So, pray for the people you will visit, for your serving partner, and for yourself.

Beyond that, make sure that you are thoroughly familiar with the ritual form that you will be leading, including its rubrics. Before you go, make the choices that are indicated—decide which scripture to read and what hymn to sing. If you are working with a partner, decide who will lead which parts. The first several times you prepare for a visit, it may help to visualize leading the various parts of the service. Having done all of that, then confirm your assignment, your appointment time, and check driving directions as necessary. Go to the church service and participate fully in it, pick up your Communion set from the person who distributes them (pastor, deacon, or Communion steward), and then make your visit. Remember that you represent Christ and the church.

Fifth Question: What Should We Do If Someone Who Is Not a Member of Our Church Asks Us for Communion?

Practically speaking, response to this question depends in part on the quantity of consecrated elements that you are carrying. If you only have enough bread and wine left for the specific person you have come to visit, then she/he must be your first priority. Otherwise, the teaching of our church pertains: "All who respond in faith to the invitation are to be welcomed." Thus, others may receive.[6]

Nevertheless, please understand that the dynamics of home Communion visits differ from those within a congregational service. If you are visiting a person in his or her private home and other persons are present, you may directly invite those others to participate in the full service, including Communion. You should also give them freedom not to participate. The situation is different in a hospital or nursing home, where privacy is at a premium. In that situation, you should focus on the person whom you have come to visit. If, however, other persons in the room specifically ask to participate in Communion, and are physically able to receive it, then you are free to include them.

Sixth Question: What about Persons With Alzheimer's Disease? Should We Give Them Communion?

Absolutely yes! As we understand it, fitness for Communion is not based on one's cognitive ability; therefore, if people with Alzheimer's are physically able to receive, they should be offered Communion.

When one engages in ritual patterns over a long period of time, they often become deeply ingrained in memory. Thus, persons in advanced stages of senility will on occasion join in a few words of a hymn or the Lord's Prayer. They may speak some other part of the liturgy. We rejoice in these moments of lucidity, however brief they may be. It is difficult to know what actually happens in such moments, but perhaps it is best simply to receive them as a gift of God. People whom you serve may not, of course, experience such a breakthrough moment, and you should not be disappointed if they do not. We minister not because people respond in any particular way, but because Christian faith demands that we not neglect people in need, especially our fellow church members. For that reason alone, we should continue to visit and share Communion with those who have Alzheimer's.

Seventh Question: What Should We Do With the Remaining Communion Elements?

Caring for elements that remain at the close of your visits should not become a major problem, since relatively small amounts of bread and juice will be placed in the Communion set. What remains—even if only a small piece of bread and a swallow of grape juice—should, however, be treated according to the classic rubrics of the church, with the respect due things that have been set apart for sacred use. Ideally, remaining elements should be consumed; after all, Jesus commanded us to eat and drink. If you have a few crumbs of bread or drops of juice, you may return these to the earth.

Do not leave remaining elements in the Communion set, where they may become moldy and stain the set. Under no circumstances should you throw remaining elements in the trash. After you have properly cared for the remaining elements, you should clean the Communion set and return it to your Communion stewards.

Eighth Question: What Happens If We Make a Mistake?

To quote Kavanagh again, "to be consumed with worry over making a liturgical mistake is the greatest mistake of all. Reverence is a virtue, not a neurosis, and God can take care of himself."[7] Kavanagh's statement was not meant as an excuse for sloppy liturgical performance. It was directed, rather, at the overly conscientious, perhaps people like you and me. You should prepare for your Communion visit and then do your best to lead it well. If you make a mistake—and you will do so from time to time—apologize if necessary, learn from it, and then move on. Justification by faith has little impact on us if we beat ourselves up every time something goes wrong.

Ninth Question: How Do We Recruit Home Communion Servers, and What Is the Proper Beginning Age for a Server?

I am convinced that public, visible practice of the Christian faith is an attractive and powerful witness, one that draws people toward ministry. Therefore, make sure to send forth the home Communion servers from the Sunday worship service itself and regularly mention their ministry in the intercessions of the church. Seeing and hearing about this work will awaken God's call in people, perhaps even in children and youth.[8] The call to service can arise from within a person, or it can come from the community. So, look for people who might make good visitors and invite them to join you for a visit. Your joy in ministry can be contagious, so give someone an opportunity to catch it.

Consider inviting youth and older, grade-school children to join you. You need, of course, to follow standard, safe sanctuary guidelines when dealing with children who are not part of your immediate family; two adults should accompany any minor. That being said, we should involve children in this and other works of ministry. It may encourage them to hear God's call.

Tenth Question: What Should We Do If Someone Calls Us in the Middle of the Night and Asks for Communion Right Then?

Since the United Methodist Church does not have a reserved sacrament, pastors must administer such emergency Communions. This would include most instances of *viaticum*, or Communion for the dying. Visits from home Communion servers will occur according to a regular schedule, as soon as possible after the congregation's celebration of the Lord's Supper. Setting such a boundary may seem overly restrictive, but it is important that people know the limitations of their office and that they cultivate an appropriate modesty about their work. There is only one God; thus, all ministry offices are limited in their scope. I am not called to save the world or to fix all of the liturgical problems in the church. I am called, rather, to teach the students I have been given and to finish this book before I move on to the next project. Such limitations encourage me to focus on manageable tasks and to do those well. Saving the world is God's problem, and fixing all of the church's liturgical problems is too large a task. Just so, as a home Communion server you should focus on the task that the church has given you. If someone requests an emergency Communion from you, then you should encourage that person to call his or her pastor, even if he or she must do so in the middle of the night. Taking such calls is part of the pastor's job.

While home Communion servers cannot provide the sacramental body of Christ in emergency situations, they should always remember that they are themselves part of the body of Christ. As the Apostle Paul wrote, "Now you are the body of Christ and individually members of it" (1 Corinthians 12:27). We receive the sacramental body to become the body of Christ in mission. So, even if home Communion servers cannot provide Communion in every instance, they can always go and be what they are, the body of Christ. They can listen carefully and serve people with compassionate love. Home Communion is but one aspect of that broader missional task.[9]

Notes

1. *The United Methodist Book of Worship* (Nashville: The United Methodist Publishing House, 1992), 36. From "A Service of Word and Table I" ©1972 The Methodist Publishing House; ©1980, 1985, 1989, 1992 The United Methodist Publishing House. Used by permission.

2. Robert Taft, "Receiving Communion—A Forgotten Symbol?" *Beyond East and West, Problems in Liturgical Understanding* (Washington, D.C., The Pastoral Press, 1984), 102.

3. Aidan Kavanagh, *Elements of Rite, A Handbook of Liturgical Style* (Collegeville: The Liturgical Press, 1982, 1990), 8. Copyright © 1982, 1990, by The Order of Saint Benedict, Inc. Published by Liturgical Press, Collegeville, MN. Reprinted with permission.

4. *The United Methodist Book of Worship* (Nashville: The United Methodist Publishing House, 1992), 51. From "A Service of Word and Table V with Persons Who Are Sick or Homebound" ©1976, 1980 by Abingdon; ©1985, 1987, 1992 The United Methodist Publishing House. Used by permission.

5. *The Book of Discipline of the United Methodist Church* (Nashville: The United Methodist Publishing House, 2004), ¶1117.9.

6. "This Holy Mystery, A United Methodist Understanding of Holy Communion," *The Book of Resolutions of the United Methodist Church*, 2004, 900. Copyright © 2004, The United Methodist Publishing House, used by permission. *The United Methodist Book of Worship*, 1992, 35, 51.

7. Aidan Kavanagh, *Elements of Rite*, 31.

8. For an example, see my book *Sacraments and Discipleship, Understanding*

Baptism and the Lord's Supper in a United Methodist Context (Nashville: Discipleship Resources, 2001), 114-15.

9. Note a broader discussion of this topic in *Sacraments and Discipleship, Understanding Baptism and the Lord's Supper in a United Methodist Context* (Nashville: Discipleship Resources, 2001), 115-117.

Appendix One:
Making Communion Sets

Home Communion sets must do the following:

- Provide an efficient way to transport the elements, vessels, and linens needed for the service;
- Protect consecrated elements from harm;
- Through the materials used and vessels chosen, point to the dignity of the sacrament;

The sets must include the following items:

- An appropriately sized container to carry the wine (or juice);
- An appropriately sized container to carry the bread;
- A single cup ("chalice"), or a container to carry the smaller individual Communion cups, for the wine (or juice);
- A small plate ("paten") for the bread;
- Communion linens, as necessary.

In order to lead the service, you will need a Bible and perhaps a hymnal. You will also need printed orders of worship and perhaps a service book (such as *The United Methodist Book of Worship*). Normally, however, these items are not carried within the Communion set itself.

One may purchase various types of home Communion sets from denominational supply houses, but they tend to be rather expensive. In addition, they do not always accommodate the practices described within this book. In particular, the small round cases in many of them are designed for holding Communion wafers and not portions of bread taken from the congregational loaf. Moreover, making home Communion sets may be another way for people in the local church to become involved in the home Communion ministry. As to making the sets, here are some thoughts on the various components.

1. When deciding upon an appropriate container to transport and protect the elements, vessels, and linens, it is best to work backwards. First, assemble the materials you will carry; then purchase or make a container that is large enough.

2. As to materials for the transport containers, consider any of the following:

    ■ Wicker baskets. (These may be handmade or purchased.)
    ■ Cloth pouches, usually with an embroidered Christian symbol. (These may be closed with a Velcro strip, a zipper, or buttons.)
    ■ Wooden boxes. (These may be handmade or purchased. Hand made ones may be built with dividers appropriate to the vessels.)
    ■ Hard clear plastic lunch boxes. (One might call this set the Tupperware® or The Container Store® special. Such sets may lack a bit aesthetically, but they may be assembled at minimal cost. If one places one of these sets on the altar, one might cover it with a white cloth or other cloth in a color appropriate to the liturgical season.)

3. For containers to transport the wine (juice), consider the following:

    ■ A container that holds from four to six ounces will suffice.
    ■ You must be able to close the container so that it does not leak.
    ■ A pour spout is ideal, so that one may pour from it into the chalice or small cups.
    ■ A small glass cruet (small glass pitcher with stopper) will work with the wicker basket set, provided you hold the basket upright at all times. You might use one of the Communion linens as a pad.
    ■ You may use medicine bottles. (They should never, of course, have been used to carry medicine).
    ■ Again, for options look to Tupperware®, The Container Store®, or discount stores. Various inexpensive vessels will suffice.

- Whatever option you choose, wash the containers after usage and replace them if they become mildewed.

4. For containers to transport the bread, consider the following:

- A container should be large enough to hold a small portion of bread torn from the congregation's loaf (a piece of about two cubic inches).
- One must be able to close and seal it.
- A simple plastic soap container will suffice. (It should never, of course, have been used to carry soap.)
- A small metal container or pouch would suffice.
- An appropriately sized zip-lock bag would also be adequate.

5. You may use simple pottery for the chalice and paten, or you may buy more expensive metal vessels.

- Remember, however, that you need to buy enough to outfit multiple sets, so spend wisely.
- Simple pottery bread plates will work quite nicely, and there is no need to purchase them from a liturgical supply house. Again, consider the discount stores. (Calling a plate a paten has been known to increase its price.)
- One might provide custom-made cloth bags to protect the chalice and paten.
- One could also wrap, or otherwise pad, the chalice and paten with some of the Communion linens.
- Plastic disposable cups work best if small cups are preferred.

6. You may purchase small, disposable Communion cups from a liturgical supply house. The following work well for transporting them:

- A simple plastic soap container. (It should never, of course, have been used to carry soap.)
- A small metal container or pouch would suffice.
- An appropriately sized zip-lock bag would also be adequate.

7. You may purchase linens or have them made to order.

- You need a small corporal, from twelve to fifteen inches square, to place under the chalice, cups, and the paten.
- You need two small purificators (essentially dinner napkins), one for the chalice and one for the paten.

- You may wish to embroider a cross on the linens.
- You may purchase linens from a liturgical supply house, but there are other, less expensive options. Always remember that purificators are napkins, and items sold as napkins can serve as purificators.

There is no one particular way to make a home Communion set, as long as you cover the basic needs. Use your imagination and see what you can do. Here is a story about what one church did for me.

I had made an appointment to take Communion to an elderly woman in my parish. She was a clergy widow who, along with her husband, had been annual conference colleagues of my grandparents. Several generations of her family were active in the church and were good friends of mine besides. We thought, "Wouldn't it be good to have a full service of Word and Table in her apartment, with family present?" So, we put it on the calendar for a weekday during Advent. When the day arrived, I prepared, gathering my Bible and my copy of *The United Methodist Book of Worship*, a small loaf of bread and bottle of juice, pewter chalice and paten in separate cloth bags, and linens. I put on my clerical collar and sat down to think about the service. As the hour approached, I loaded everything into a brown paper grocery bag and drove to my appointment.

When I arrived, she and several family members were present. I found my seat and a flat surface on which to place the various items. I unrolled the top of the now rumpled shopping bag and began extracting the various items from it. "Ah, let's see . . . the books . . . then the vessels, and now, yes . . . the bread and juice . . . the linens . . . there, now we're ready." Watching this spectacle unfold, her granddaughter-in-law sitting next to me commented, in a hushed voice, "I thought we were going to see the magic umbrella come out next." Indeed, my paper shopping bag was not dignified enough.

Taking pity on this aesthetic dullard, a parishioner showed up in my office a few weeks later, took measurements on my vessels, my Bible and service book, and commissioned a local furniture builder to fashion a handsome and sturdy wooden box for use on such visits. May you be blessed with such compassionate and creative friends.

Appendix Two:
Order for Servers

An Order for Use in Extended Table Services (Server's Copy)

The following portions are reprinted from The United Methodist Book of Worship, *copyright ©1992 by the United Methodist Publishing House: Opening Prayer, Invitation, Confession and Pardon, and Prayer after Communion. Used by permission.*

This ministry of the extended table, and the Order of Worship presented here, is conducted under the rites and rubrics of the United Methodist Church. It is endorsed by the Administrative Board of (this congregation) and occurs under the supervision of (our pastoral staff).

INTRODUCTORY RUBRICS

1. First dismissal scenario from the congregation's Service of Word and Table: The Communion sets will be given to you, perhaps by a deacon or Communion steward, after the congregation has received Communion and before the prayer after Communion. You will be dismissed to your visit and will depart while the congregation sings its final hymn.

2. Second dismissal scenario: Retrieve the elements after the congregational service and proceed to the visit as soon as possible.

3. Under either dismissal scenario, the Communion sets will be prepared for you, and they should include an adequate supply of the

consecrated elements. If you think that you will need more than the usual amount, please notify the stewards ahead of time. Should you find yourself with an inadequate supply of consecrated elements, please notify the pastor. Under no circumstances should you serve unconsecrated elements, nor should you consecrate them yourself.

4. When you arrive at the visit site, greet your host as you enter his or her home or room. Find a table or flat surface (perhaps a coffee table, an end table, or even a TV tray) on which you can arrange the elements for the service. Set up for the service, putting the bread on the plate and small amounts of wine (or juice) in the cups.

5. You may converse some before the service begins, but you should try to keep such conversation to a minimum. Seek to begin the service as soon as possible after you arrive.

SERVICE OF THE WORD

Greeting
Give the following signal that the service is beginning.
Grace to you, and peace, in Jesus Christ our Lord. Amen.
This morning in our worship service, we celebrated the service of the Lord's Supper. We've come to bring you Communion from the same altar.

Opening Prayer
Invite those present to join in the prayer, and at least in the "Amen."
Almighty God, to you all hearts are open, all desires known, and from you no secrets are hidden. Cleanse the thoughts of our hearts by the inspiration of your Holy Spirit, that we may perfectly love you, and worthily magnify your holy name, through Christ our Lord. Amen.[1]

Act of Praise
Sing or recite a verse (or verses) of a hymn or Psalm.

Scripture
Read one of the scriptures from the morning (Epistle or Gospel), introducing the reading with the following statement:
This morning we read from _____.
The leader or others present may offer comments on the lesson.

Prayer of Intercession

Offer a brief prayer for the person whom you are visiting. Also offer any concerns he or she may wish to raise. Encourage him or her to speak prayers as well.

SERVICE OF COMMUNION

Invitation
The leader says the following:
Christ our Lord invites to his table all who love him and seek to grow into his likeness. Let us draw near with faith, make our humble confession, and prepare to receive this Holy Sacrament.[2]

Confession and Pardon
Invite those present to join in the entire prayer, and at least in the "Amen."

> **We do not presume to come to this your table, merciful Lord, trusting in our own goodness, but in your unfailing mercies. We are not worthy that you should receive us, but give your word and we shall be healed, through Jesus Christ our Lord. Amen.[3]**

The leader continues as follows:
Hear the good news: Christ died for us while we were yet sinners; that is proof of God's love toward us. In the name of Jesus Christ, you are forgiven![4]

The Peace
Signs and words of God's peace are exchanged.[5]
The peace of the Lord be with you.

The Lord's Prayer
The leader says the following, joined by the others present:
Before we receive Communion, let us pray together as Jesus taught us saying, "**Our Father . . .**"

Giving the Bread and Cup
Serve all present who wish to receive. At the least, the home Communion servers should receive with the homebound member.

What if you have a shortage of Communion cups, or of wine (juice)? For example, say that you have five small cups but seven persons who wish to receive. In that case, some may receive by intinction. The principal recipient of the visit, however, should be served first and should have a cup of his or her own.

Administer the elements with the following or similar words:
The body of Christ, given for you. **Amen.**
The blood of Christ, given for you. **Amen.**[6]

Prayer After Communion
The leader prays as follows:

Most bountiful God, we give you thanks for the world you have created, for the gift of life, and for giving yourself to us in Jesus Christ, whose holy life, suffering and death, and glorious resurrection have delivered us from slavery to sin and death. We thank you that in the power of your Holy Spirit you have fed us in this Sacrament, united us with Christ, and given us a foretaste of your heavenly banquet. We are your children, and yours is the glory, now and for ever; through Jesus Christ our Lord. **Amen.**[7]

Blessing

The leader addresses those gathered with the following words:

The grace of the Lord Jesus Christ, and the love of God, and the communion of the Holy Spirit be with you. **Amen.**[8]

RUBRICS FOLLOWING THE SERVICE

1. If it seems appropriate, spend a few moments in conversation.

2. When your visits for the day are completed, consume any unused elements. A small amount of wine (juice) and crumbs may be returned to the earth, perhaps in your flowerbed. Consecrated Communion elements should not be thrown in the trash.

3. Please report completed visits on the form provided.

ADDITIONAL RUBRICS

1. Always remember that you are a guest in someone else's home. If someone hesitates to receive this ministry from you, remind him or her that your ministry is endorsed by your congregation and supervised by your pastor. If communicants still refuse to receive you, do not argue with them. Please let your pastor know about any such refusals.

2. Since we do not recognize a reserved sacrament in the United Methodist Church, you should plan to make your visits on the day of the congregational service or on the next day at the very least.

3. Schedule home visits ahead of time. It is a good idea to call ahead when planning to visit in nursing homes. It is possible that other activities have been scheduled at the time you hope to visit.

4. Observe hospital visiting hours.

5. Serve only the consecrated elements given to you at the congregational service. Using unconsecrated elements, or laypersons attempting to consecrate more, violates the trust on which this ministry is based.

6. Preserve confidentiality. You may, however, share information with your pastor. If you see evidence of abuse or neglect, inform your pastor immediately.

7. Above all, remember that you represent Christ and this church. Go prayerfully, in Christ's joy and peace.

Notes

1. *The United Methodist Hymnal* (Nashville: The United Methodist Publishing House, 1989), 6. From "A Service of Word and Table I" © 1972, 1980, 1985, 1989, The United Methodist Publishing House. Used by permission.

2. *The United Methodist Book of Worship* (Nashville: The United Methodist Publishing House, 1992), 51. From "A Service of Word and Table V with Persons Who Are Sick or Homebound" ©1976, 1980 by Abingdon; ©1985, 1987, 1992 The United Methodist Publishing House. Used by permission.

3. Ibid. Used by permission.

4. Ibid., 52. Used by permission.

5. Ibid. Used by permission.

6. Ibid., 53. Used by permission.

7. *The United Methodist Book of Worship*, 1992, 53. Used by permission.

8. *The United Methodist Book of Worship* (Nashville: The United Methodist Publishing House, 1992), 53. From "A Service of Word and Table V with Persons Who Are Sick or Homebound" ©1976, 1980 by Abingdon; ©1985, 1987, 1992 The United Methodist Publishing House. Used by permission.

Appendix Three:
Order for Those Visited

An Order for Use in Home Communion Services

The following portions are reprinted from The United Methodist Book of Worship, *copyright ©1992 by the United Methodist Publishing House: Opening Prayer, Invitation, Confession and Pardon, and Prayer after Communion. Used by permission.*

This ministry of the extended table, and the Order of Worship presented here, is conducted under the rites and rubrics of the United Methodist Church. It is endorsed by the Administrative Board of (this congregation) and occurs under the supervision of (our pastoral staff).

Service of the Word

Greeting
Opening Prayer

> Almighty God, to you all hearts are open, all desires known, and from you no secrets are hidden. Cleanse the thoughts of our hearts by the inspiration of your Holy Spirit, that we may perfectly love you, and worthily magnify your holy name, through Christ our Lord. Amen.[1]

Act of Praise
Scripture

Prayer of Confession

SERVICE OF COMMUNION

Invitation
Confession and Pardon

> We do not presume to come to this your table, merciful Lord, trusting in our own goodness, but in your unfailing mercies. We are not worthy that you should receive us, but give your word and we shall be healed, through Jesus Christ our Lord. Amen.[2]

The Peace
The Lord's Prayer
Giving the Bread and Cup
Prayer After Communion

> Most bountiful God, we give you thanks for the world you have created, for the gift of life, and for giving yourself to us in Jesus Christ, whose holy life, suffering and death, and glorious resurrection have delivered us from slavery to sin and death. We thank you that in the power of your Holy Spirit you have fed us in this Sacrament, united us with Christ, and given us a foretaste of your heavenly banquet. We are your children, and yours is the glory, now and for ever; through Jesus Christ our Lord. **Amen.**[3]

BLESSING

Notes

1. *The United Methodist Hymnal* (Nashville: The United Methodist Publishing House, 1989), 6. From "A Service of Word and Table I" © 1972, 1980, 1985, 1989, The United Methodist Publishing House. Used by permission.

2. *The United Methodist Book of Worship* (Nashville: The United Methodist Publishing House, 1992), 51. From "A Service of Word and Table V with Persons Who Are Sick or Homebound" ©1976, 1980 by Abingdon; ©1985, 1987, 1992 The United Methodist Publishing House. Used by permission.

3. Ibid., 53. Used by permission.

Appendix Four:
Visitation Report

Home Communion Visitation Report
(Please return to the visitation captain)

Visitation Team: _____

Person(s) visited: _____

Place visited: _____

Date/Time of visit: _____

Did you learn anything that the pastor should know? (Please describe details below and on the reverse side.)